Seaport to Seaside

Lines to Southport and Ormskirk –
13 decades of trains and travel

by

John W. Gahan

Cover Design: ERIC. R. MONKS

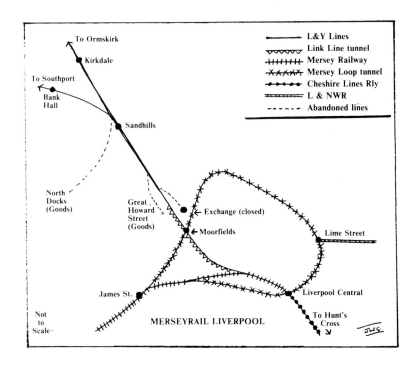

Key to map opposite

L&Y lines electrified (as at 1923)

L&Y lines non-electrified

Cheshire Lines Railway

Midland Railway

London & North Western Railway

Liverpool Overhead Railway (Stations not shown)

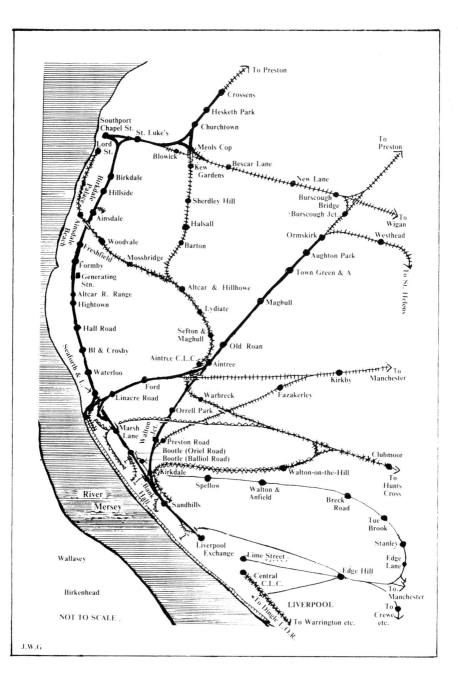

To Preston

Crossens

Hesketh Park

Churchtown

Southport
Chapel St.
St. Luke's
Lord
St.
Blowick
Meols Cop

Kew
Gardens

Bescar Lane

To
Preston

Birkdale

Hillside

Ainsdale

Woodvale

Freshfield

Formby

Generating
Stn.

Altcar R. Range

Hightown

Sherdley Hill

Halsall

Barton

Mossbridge

Altcar & Hillhowe

Lydiate

Sefton &
Maghull

New Lane

Burscough
Bridge
Burscough Jct.

To
Wigan

Westhead

Ormskirk

Aughton Park

Town Green & A

Maghull

To St. Helens

Birkdale Palace

Ainsdale Beach

Hall Road

Bl & Crosby

Waterloo

Seaforth & L.

Aintree C.L.C.

Old Roan

Aintree

Ford

Linacre Road

Marsh
Lane

Walton Jct.

Preston Road
Bootle (Oriel Road)
Bootle (Balliol Road)

Kirkdale

Warbreck

Orrell Park

Spellow

Fazakerley

Kirkby

To
Manchester

Clubmoor

To
Hunts
Cross

Walton-on-the-Hill

Walton &
Anfield

Breck
Road

Tue
Brook

Stanley

Edge
Lane

River
Mersey

Bank Hall

Sandhills

Wallasey

Birkenhead

NOT TO SCALE.

Liverpool
Exchange

Lime Street

Central
C.L.C.

To Dingle L.O.R.

To Warrington etc.

Edge Hill

LIVERPOOL

To
Manchester

To
Crewe
etc.

J.W.G

By the same author:

Seventeen Stations to Dingle — the Liverpool Overhead Railway remembered.

The Line Beneath the Liners — A hundred years of Mersey Railway sights and sounds.

Steel Wheels to Deeside — the Wirral Railway past and present.

First published 1985 by Countyvise Limited, 1 & 3 Grove Road, Rock Ferry, Birkenhead, Wirral, Merseyside L42 3XS . . . .
. . . . ISBN 0 907768 07 5

and

Avon AngliA Publications & Services, Annesley House, 21 Southside, Weston-super-Mare, Avon BS23 2QU . . . .
. . . . ISBN 0 905466 73 X

Photoset and printed by Birkenhead Press Limited, 1 & 3 Grove Road, Rock Ferry, Birkenhead, Wirral, Merseyside L42 3XS.

Introduction

Few of today's travellers on the busy electric lines to the districts North of Liverpool will have heard of the Liverpool, Crosby & Southport and the Liverpool, Ormskirk & Preston Railways, but way back in the now remote 1840's these were the forerunners of the present-day Southport and Ormskirk lines of Merseyrail. Both systems soon passed into the net of the Lancashire & Yorkshire Railway which operated them until the Grouping of 1923 when the L & Y became part of the far-flung London, Midland & Scottish Railway. Finally, in 1948 the lines became part of the nationalised British Railways, London Midland Region.

The Southport line was electrified as early as 1904, being Britain's first main-line electrification, whilst the electrification of the line to Ormskirk was carried out in stages up to 1913. Both lines were instrumental in developing the residential districts along the coast, and inland, though the Ormskirk line was not as successful as that to Southport in this respect.

Threatened with closure during the Beeching era, the Southport line eventually escaped extinction and is now a vital component of Merseyside's passenger transport system. The Ormskirk line was not considered for closure, as at the time it carried passenger trains to various destinations further North, also some goods traffic but things changed soon after, and the line beyond Ormskirk now sees only a limited service of diesel trains on the section as far as Preston.

Extensions to the electrified lines in more recent times have greatly increased their usefulness, which is reflected in the enormous numbers of people now travelling on the trains. There is however, some cause for regret in the demise of Liverpool Exchange station, from which the rail traveller could reach North Lancashire towns and the Fylde coast, among other destinations, more conveniently than at present. The electric trains, which threaded their way though a maze of lines near Exchange now go unobtrusively underground, whilst the once busy and polished rails that carried electric, steam and diesel trains for so many years have vanished completely. Sic Transit Gloria.

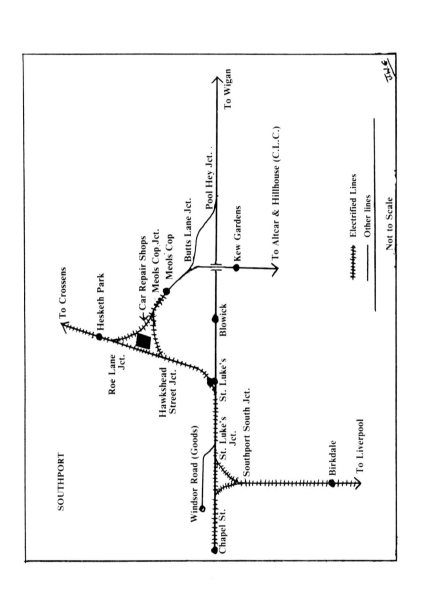

Southport Train

Liverpool Exchange — industry surrounded,
Mills, factories, streets and houses.
Signal lights, red and green,
Trains — electric, diesel, steam.
Warehouses, tunnels, bridges, rails,
Rows of wagons, goods and mails.
Coal, tobacco, oil, cement,
Freight from every continent,
Sandhills, there are none to see,
Bank Hall, place of industry.
Bootle, port of ships and cranes,
Marsh Lane, gasworks, passing trains.
Seaforth, busy landscape spread —
Late, lamented "overhead".
Waterloo, passed at last,
Steel wheels rolling fast.
Crosby, residential place,
Presents a nicely pleasant face,
Hall Road station lies ahead,
Countryside, carriage shed.
Hightown, sand dunes, fields and trees,
Formby by the open seas.
Freshfield, long road to the beach,
Ainsdale, station on the street.
Hillside, houses all around,
Level crossings now abound.
Birkdale, Southport's Southern door,
The train is nearly home once more.
Southport Junction soon is reached —
Journey's end at Chapel Street.

J.W.G.

Iron Horses for Merchant Princes

It is almost impossible to deal with the recent history of Britain's railways without making reference to the famous "Beeching Report" of 1963, that controversial document that delighted the road transport and motoring interests whilst striking despondency into the hearts of those to whom the railway was not only a travel medium but a part of life itself. It was a gloomy report notwithstanding its proposals for development in certain directions, but the main theme was closure and abandonment of many railway lines and train services. It is true that a large number of the lines proposed for closure served rural or thinly populated districts, but there were some included that were far from being country branches or thinly-trafficked arteries of lost commerce. Foremost among the last mentioned type of line was the efficient and popular Liverpool to Southport electric railway. The potential closure of this busy line was the cause of widespread consternation and volumes of indignant protest, for the "Southport Line" as it is locally known, serves a populous residential area and is heavily used, about 10,000 passengers per day travelling upon it at the time of the "Beeching Report", and the possibility of it meeting a similar fate to that of the late, lamented Liverpool Overhead Railway, closed in 1956, aroused public ire in no uncertain fashion!

The Southport Line was recommended for closure because it no longer covered its operating costs. In common with suburban railways in most parts of the World it carries an enormous volume of peak-hour traffic necessitating extra trains, staff and track capacity that are idle for the greater part of the day, a problem which is extremely difficult to resolve. Nevertheless, the numbers of passengers travelling on the line during the off-peak hours was still sufficient to necessitate a frequent service, and trains hummed to and fro over its brightly polished rails at brief intervals all day long. Even the most ardent of railway abolishonists of the early 1960's were inclined to admit that this busy railway was likely to be retained for many years to come — even if other lines on Merseyside were closed, due to the slim prospect of any alternative transport medium being able to equal the trains for speed and efficiency in mass transportation, two factors that accounted for the popularity of the Southport Line. The possibility of the disappearance of this well used and obviously valuable railway aroused a great deal of resentment among its thousands of daily travellers, and was quite a blow to the good relations which had been maintained for very many years between passengers and railway companies — the Lancashire & Yorkshire followed by the London Midland & Scottish, and inherited by British Railways. More especially was the proposed closure a dismaying prospect because it was promulgated under

Nationalisation, which everyone believed was for the public benefit, and no official regrets were expressed — the line was to be simply discarded without regard to the provision of adequate alternatives (if indeed such could be found) and with no thoughts about future consequences — and this at a time when traffic hold-ups on Liverpool's streets were causing untold hours of delay!

A widely supported campaign for the retention of the Liverpool-Southport railway was put into force by affected parties and the battle raged for about two years before the threat of closure was removed, pending official investigations into the future transport requirements of Merseyside, in which the line clearly had important potentialities. Its demise was unthinkable even as it stood, quite apart from what it could become if linked to other local lines, possibilities in this direction having since been realised, of which more later.

The story of the railway between the great Mersey port and the completely contrasting resort of Southport 18 miles distant is one of progress from its humble beginning as a short local line, its later absorption by a larger undertaking, and its fame in becoming the first section of a British main-line railway to be converted from steam to electric traction. It is a relief to turn one's back on the gloomy, politically bedevilled railway scene of the last 35 years and look instead at the beginning when railways were new and had a golden age ahead of them, when nobody thought that a time would come when they would be abolished almost with the same fervour with which they had been built!

The progress of Liverpool after it had begun to outgrow its fishing village status was slow at first, but began to gain more rapid impetus from about the 1830's, though this progress brought blight as well as prosperity. Many of the affluent merchants and manufacturers who had set the wheels of progress turning, and new recruits to their ranks, having established themselves in large, handsome residences in various districts that were, at the time, on the fringes of the town and far enough from the overcrowding, smoke and insanitary streets to permit of gracious living, eventually found that they were gradually becoming surrounded by the tide of the town's expansion. Consequently they began to search for alternative places in which to make their abode, as far away as they could get from their centres of business, yet within reasonable travelling distance of the town which was beginning to feel the strain of an unceasing influx of new inhabitants. The scene was quickly changing from one of semi-rural tranquility to a hurly-burly of commerce and industry, and was no longer a place in which living could be enjoyed. Unlike the rank and file of men and women who served the industries and shipping, the commercial gentlemen could afford to move, and most of them did so, having no wish to be surrounded by the hustle and bustle, smoke

11

and grime inseparable from progress, and fine Georgian houses, vacated one by one gradually descended to the role of providing accommodation for humbler tenants, whilst already grim slum conditions increased as the number of immigrants moving-in outstripped the rate of house construction.

The men of commerce, discomfited by events, began to look with increasing favour on the surrounding countryside and along the coast to the North of Liverpool to build new homes where the air was fresh and healthy breezes blew in from the wide expanses of the Irish Sea. Many of the "Merchant Princes" moved out as far afield as Southport, at that time a small but promising resort which small numbers of pleasure seekers visited during the Summer months, making their journeys in stage coaches or in their own carriages. The stage coach services were infrequent however. In 1833 a coach left Liverpool at 4.00 p.m. on weekdays — it ran in connection with the 2.00 p.m. train from Manchester. In the opposite direction the coach left Southport in time to connect at Liverpool with the 12.00 p.m. Manchester train. By 1839 there were four coaches daily from Liverpool to Southport in Winter and eight in the Summer months, Sundays excepted. The aristocrat of the service, "The Eclipse", departed from the Crown Inn, Red Cross Street at 3.00 p.m. for Southport via Ormskirk, returning from Southport next day at 8.00 a.m. This vehicle was advertised as an "elegant light posting coach", indeed a veritable greyhound of the highway!

In addition to the stage coaches, passenger-carrying boats plied on the Leeds & Liverpool canal, sailing as far as Scarisbrick, which is only four miles from Southport, passengers transferring to coaches for the balance of the journey. This was a time-consuming process however, and not one that attracted huge crowds. The boats were, of course, hauled by horses plodding slowly along the towpath.

The land adjacent to the coast between Liverpool and Southport was a sparsely populated, marshy and wind-swept wilderness in the mid-nineteenth century — nothing had changed in years except that the coastline was gradually eroding, a state of affairs that was soon taken in hand once the area had begun to become inhabited. The marshes were gradually drained, and erosion halted by the planting of Starr grass on the sand-hills. Today the coastal area is extremely attractive, with pine woods, cultivated fields and golf courses interspersing pleasant residential districts, and is a favourite venue for pleasure seekers and sportsmen. As a matter of fact the sea has performed an about-turn in recent years and left vast tracts of sandy beaches at the Southport end of the Mersey estuary.

It was the development of the land for residential purposes that led to proposals, first heard in the late 1830's, for a railway between Liverpool and Southport. Every day large numbers of horse-drawn vehicles of a wide and fascinating variety, carrying the men of commerce, converged on the town of Liverpool whilst many of them rode their own steeds, and congestion in the streets, which added to the inconvenience and slowness of such transport media naturally led to demands for railways as soon as this newer mode became reliable, as exemplified by the Liverpool & Manchester line. Unlike the latter, which carried a heavy goods traffic, the proposed Southport railway was to be primarily a passenger facility and it was perhaps for this reason it did not interest manufacturers and tradesmen so much as a scheme for lines linking industrial centres would have done, and in any case, there were few manufactures in Liverpool in the 1830's, the town being mainly concerned with shipping and commerce. Capital had largely to be raised among local businessmen and this took time. The first definite scheme for a Liverpool-Southport line was initiated by the Liverpool & Bury Railway Company, which published the following notice in the "Liverpool Mercury" of 25th July, 1845:

LIVERPOOL CROSBY & FORMBY RAILWAY
Preliminary Announcement.

This railway is intended to open up a more expeditious communication between Liverpool and the rapidly improving and populous districts lying to the North on the Eastern banks of the River Mersey. The line starts from a point upon the proposed Liverpool & Bury Railway, at or near the Sandhills bridge on the Leeds and Liverpool Canal, and proceeds by Bootle, Seaforth, Litherland, Waterloo, Great and Little Crosby to Formby, from which point it is proposed to obtain Powers to form an extension to Southport should it hereafter be deemed desirable.

A detailed Prospectus, with a list of Provisional Committee will be published in a few days; in the meantime all communications to be addressed to Messrs Brebner and Haigh, Solicitors, Liverpool.

This particular scheme did not materialise, but in August, 1846 another notice appeared in the "Liverpool Mercury" regarding a new railway project, as follows:

LIVERPOOL, CROSBY AND SOUTHPORT RAILWAY
Preliminary Announcement.

A company for constructing the above railway is in course of formation and for affording to the districts along the coast a cheap and easy communication with Liverpool.

The landowners have been communicated with and are generally favourable; and their wishes will be consulted as far as possible as to the course of the line.

A detailed Prospectus will shortly be issued, and communications may in the meantime be addressed to Messrs H. and W. Toogood, Solicitors, 22 Parliament Street, London.

Liverpool 28th August, 1846.

13

The Secretary of the company was James C. Duncan and the head office was established at No. 2 Exchange Street West, Liverpool.

The first meeting of the company was held in Liverpool on 6th October, 1846. The plan originally envisaged was for the line to take its course through Bootle, Seaforth, Waterloo, Crosby, Altcar, Formby, Downholland, Halsall, Raven Meols and Birkdale, terminating near Chapel Street in Southport. This plan was opposed by the Blundell families who were owners of large estates in the district but they gave some land gratis when the promoters agreed to take the line through Crosby nearer the coast. Following upon the aforementioned meeting, a lengthy notice appeared in "Herapaths Railway Journal" for 24th October, 1846:

LIVERPOOL, CROSBY AND SOUTHPORT RAILWAY

Registered Provisionally.
Capital £150,000.
In 7,500 shares of £20 each – Deposit £2 per share.
Provisional Directors (with power to add to their number).
William Blundell Esq., Crosby Hall. Chairman.
William Nichol Esq., Liverpool. Vice Chairman.
James Aiken Esq., Liverpool.
Henry Cleaver Chapman Esq.
Thomas Chilton Esq.
William Earle Esq.
Eyre Evans Esq.
Richard Formby Esq.
Robertson Gladstone Esq.
George Holt Esq.
Hugh Hornby Esq.
Cottingham Moss Esq.
William Potter Esq.
Emanuel Zwilchenbart Esq.

Committee of Management...
William Blundell Esq., Chairman.
Robertson Gladstone Esq.
Hugh Hornby Esq.
William Potter Esq.

Engineers...
George Stephenson Esq.
C.P. Bidder Esq.

Solicitors...
Messrs Duncan and Radcliffe, Liverpool.
Messrs H. and W. Toogood, 22 Parliament Street, London.

Bankers...
Liverpool – Messrs Moss and Co.
Manchester – Messrs Wm. Jones, Loyds, and Co.
London – Messrs Barclay and Co.

Prospectus.

The object of this Company is to construct a line of railway between Liverpool, Crosby and Southport. The accommodation proposed to be thus given has long been desired, but the difficulty of obtaining a convenient entrance into Liverpool has until lately proved an unsurmountable obstacle. This obstacle the Liverpool & Bury Railway, now in course of construction, affords the means of overcoming, it being proposed by the present scheme to make use of that line for nearly a mile and a half out of Liverpool, and thence proceed by way of Bootle, Seaforth, Waterloo, Crosby, and along the coast through Formby, to Southport, affording to those places and the adjacent farm districts a cheap and speedy means of communication with Liverpool. On the other hand, the benefits to the overcrowded population of Liverpool in a sanitary point of view, by giving ready access to the rapidly increasing bathing places along the coast, the district of Crosby, and the much frequented and salubrious watering place of Southport, as well as throwing open the intermediate country for the purpose of villas and residences, cannot well be over-estimated.

The undertaking is promoted by the principal Landowners and other parties locally interested.

The line is about sixteen miles in length, and being nearly level, is entirely free from engineering difficulties. A considerable part of the land between Crosby and Southport, over which it will pass, has already been given by the Landowners, and the cost of construction will be unusually small.

The liability of each shareholder will be restricted by Act of Parliament, to the amount of his Subscription, and Powers will be applied for in the Bill to allow interest at £4 per cent on all calls from the passing of the Act until the opening of the line. Application for Shares may be made in the subjoined form, on or before the 6th of November next, to the Solicitors or to any of the following Sharebrokers ... Messrs D. and J.B. Neilson, or Messrs Aspinall and Hughes, Liverpool; Robert McEwen, Esq., Manchester; or to Messrs Hill, Fawcett, and Hill, 29 Threadneedle Street, London.

Several schemes for new railways in South Lancashire were placed before Parliament during 1846. The Liverpool, Crosby & Southport Company was opposed by the East Lancashire Railway and five other parties, but nevertheless, the Bill was passed on 2nd July, 1847. Among the provisions of the Act was one stipulating that the bridge required over the River Alt at Formby be constructed to the satisfaction of the Admiralty, and must be capable of permitting the escape of flood water. There were to be twelve level crossings between Sandhills and Southport — two in Bootle, one in Litherland, two in Great Crosby, three in Formby, two in Birkdale and two in North Meols (Southport).

It will be noted that one of the Chief Engineers for the Southport line was the famous George Stephenson, who having left Liverpool in 1833, returned to the scene of his earlier triumphs. In comparison with the pioneer Liverpool & Manchester line, that to Southport was a simple task to build. He had no long tunnels, towering viaducts or deep cuttings to construct, and no bitter parliamentary battles to fight. He had been widely travelled and had engineered several railways since he was last in Liverpool, so building the line to Southport was almost child's play to him and his partner, C.P. Bidder. Stephenson also assisted with the construction of the Liverpool, Ormskirk & Preston Railway, but the latter included a lengthy tunnel and some problems with marshland.

Nothing was done about commencing work on the line for some time after the Parliamentary Act had been passed, but on 1st January, 1848 the Clarendon Rooms in North John Street, Liverpool, were the venue for a meeting of the Company, with William Blundell as Chairman, at which it was resolved to commence construction without any further delay, the section of line between Waterloo and Southport to be tackled first. Thereafter there was little talk and plenty of action, so much so, that only four months elapsed between the cutting of the first piece of turf, which took place at Waterloo on 24th March, 1848, and the completion of the line (which was single) all the way to Southport, a distance of 13 miles.

The Contractors who built the Southport railway were Messrs McCormick & Holme, of Liverpool, who were also engaged on construction of the Liverpool & Bury Railway, and great credit was their due for the speedy and expeditious manner in which they tackled and completed the job. Though no longer a novelty by the late 1840's, railway construction had its problems, depending on location and type of terrain through which projected lines were to make their way — some were easy, others were extremely difficult. There were very few problems with the Liverpool-Southport line however. Much had been learned since the first task of this nature — the construction of the Liverpool & Manchester Railway, had been successfully completed, and there were massive railway works either completed or in progress elsewhere in the country. Nevertheless, to construct a railway 13 miles in length in such a short time was a notable achievement. Doubtless directors, contractors and others concerned with the new railway schemes studied the Liverpool & Manchester, which was a prime example of the engineer's triumph over obstacles, natural and otherwise, and used it as an object lesson in successful railway management, learning much that would be of value in their new venture into the realms of mechanical transport.

By 1846 however, the L & M had been merged with the Grand Junction Railway and it was possible to travel by rail from Liverpool to London, but not yet between Liverpool and Southport.

Sir William Forwood, one of Liverpool's most prominent leading citizens of yesteryear tells us, in his book "Recollections of a Busy Life", of an inspection trip made over the line by a group of directors who travelled from Waterloo to Hightown in two First class carriages which were drawn by three grey horses, driven by a man seated on the top of the leading vehicle. Such a proceeding can scarcely by imagined by today's passengers as the electric trains sweep speedily and effortlessly along the stretch of track over which the hardy directors made their sedate trip so long ago!

The public opening of the Liverpool, Crosby & Southport Railway took place on 24th July, 1848, being an occasion of rejoicing and celebration at Waterloo, Southport and the intermediate villages. The proceedings were not of course, anything like so grand as those which accompanied the opening of the Liverpool & Manchester Railway 18 years previously. Like the L & M the LC & S was a *Liverpool* railway, even if its rails did not yet enter the precincts of the town, and as such, was considered worthy of a suitable inauguration ceremony, but nobility was absent — no Dukes rode in special trains and few VIP's appear to have been present. The proceedings and festivities were somewhat dampened by heavy rain which fell all morning, but it did not kill the enthusiasm of the local populations. Horse-drawn omnibuses laden with spectators arrived at Waterloo station one after the other, the station itself being gaily decorated for the occasion.

A train departed for Southport at 10.00 a.m. and returned soon after 11.00 a.m. with the band of the Oddfellows Society and everyone else who could get aboard. At 2.35 p.m. the Official opening train, consisting of 16 carriages packed solid with passengers pulled out for Southport amid cheers and hurrah's from the crowd. The "Liverpool Mercury" reported favourably on the smooth riding of the carriages in comparison with those on other railways. A large number of people awaited the arrival of the train at Southport and by the time it had pulled in, the sun was shining in all its glory and flags on various buildings had dried out sufficiently to flutter in the breeze. The "Liverpool Mercury" had this to say... "We hope ere long to see the land along the railroad studded with beautiful villas surrounded by the richest foliage in which the 'Merchant Princes' of this great mart of commerce may spend their leisure hours in ease and enjoyment". This they certainly did! In due course the "Princes" were followed by less-wealthy people who settled in the intermediate villages, resulting in their expansion and development into quite large communities.

At the time of the railway's completion the company had only three locomotives, none of which proved suitable for the work which they had to perform. They were numbered 1, 2 and 3, being named respectively "Blundell", "Formby", and "Sefton". Of these "Sefton" had the honour of hauling the first train on the opening day of the railway. All were outside-cylindered 0-4-2's built by Tayleur & Company at Newton-le-Willows in 1848. None of these engines lasted long on the Southport line as they were of insufficient power and were soon sold. "Sefton" left the line in 1850, "Blundell" and "Formby" following in 1854. Five other locomotives were obtained in due course, as follows: No. 4 "Waterloo" of the 2-2-2 type with outside cylinders, built by Robert Stephenson & Company in 1848, and later rebuilt. This engine came second-hand from the Norfolk Railway in East Anglia. No. 5 "Southport" was of the same type and from the same builders as No. 4 and was also ex-Norfolk Railway. Engine No. 6 "Firefly" was a 2-2-2 with inside cylinders, built by Sharp Stewart & Company in 1849. Two more locomotives, the numbers of which are not definitely known were named "England" and "Spitfire". Both were 2-2-2's with inside cylinders. "England" was built by George England & Company at the Hatcham Ironworks, London, in 1849 , whilst "Spitfire" was built locally by George Forrester & Company of Vauxhall Road Foundry, Liverpool in 1850.

As no connection existed between the Southport line and any other railway at the time, all the locomotives needed to be transported from Liverpool on road waggons drawn by straining horse teams. The route followed to Waterloo station was via the Crosby Road and finally along a sandy lane in which the waggons sometimes sank down to their axles, and it was long, hard back-breaking work to get them out, as it was also to get the locomotives unloaded and safely onto the firmness of the newly laid railway track.

A small shed in which to house and service the locomotives was built at Waterloo, a short distance to the South of the passenger station on the seaward side of the line, but when the railway was later continued to Sandhills the extension was made from the North end of the station near what became St. John's Road, and a new shed for the engines was built on land which today is occupied by the electric sub-station, on the East side of the line just North of South Road bridge. The site of the original station became a goods and mineral depot. At Southport another engine shed was built after the line had been extended to Chapel Street, predecessor of the large and busy locomotive depot that was established on a different site at a later date.

One of the most interesting features of the railway, and one of which the company was extremely proud was the electric telegraph system, which not only fulfilled the function of expediting train operations but was also useful in relaying to Liverpool messages from ships in the Crosby Channel, particularly from any that may have been in difficulties, or run aground on Burbo Bank, a fairly frequent occurence in those far off days of non-mechanical navigation. The system was installed by the Magnetic Telegraph Company, at first only between Waterloo and Southport, but in 1855 it was extended into Liverpool. The little LC & S was indeed abreast of the times!

In spite of having several wealthy directors, the small company was soon in financial difficulties and life became a continual struggle. Traffic was thin in view of the sparse population and the railway had to develop the land before there was any prospect of heavy traffic. The situation became so acute that the directors were reluctant to permit the continuation of the railway towards Liverpool until the existing liabilities had been met. It is of interest to note that the wages bill for the first six months (excepting the Secretary's salary) amounted to £52 and the company hoped to reduce this!

It was not until July, 1849, that the go-ahead was given for the construction of the extension to Sandhills, this to be of double track. The work entailed a cutting near Waterloo, and an embankment from Marsh Lane through Bootle. There were also a couple of level crossings on this stretch of line, and a bridge over the Leeds & Liverpool Canal had to be built at Bootle. The line was completed by October, 1850, of which more later.

For a period of little more than two years, passengers were conveyed between Tithebarn Street, Liverpool, and Waterloo in horsedrawn omnibuses operated by Daniel Busby, a pioneer of local passenger transport on Merseyside. No less than 74 trips per day were run (far more than there were trains), with an average of 14 passengers per journey. When the Liverpool Crosby & Southport Railway Company established a booking office at the corner of North John Street and Dale Street the omnibus service was extended to this location. Not only did a service operate to and from Waterloo; there were also 22 trips per day to and from Seaforth. During the first six months complaints were frequently made regarding the shortage of accommodation on the omnibuses, but this was soon remedied. First class passengers could obtain a through ticket covering the road and rail journey, but Third class travellers were obliged to book twice, at road and railway stations.

In the first couple of months of operation passenger traffic figures were quite gratifying, although trains were few. The following item from the "Liverpool Mercury" of 12th September, 1848 gives some idea of the popularity of the new railway:—

"Railway Traffic. As we have stated elsewhere, the number of passengers upon the railway for the last few days has been exceptionally great. Between Monday and Thursday upwards of

thirteen hundred were booked at the station, and at Waterloo there were a still greater number. Besides three hundred day tickets that were issued at that station on Wednesday and Thursday. The numbers leaving there on Thursday evening was more than all the carriages at this end could contain; for although every carriage and every luggage van (with the guard's accommodation attached) were completely stowed, it was necessary to await the arrival of another extra train, or 'train extraordinary' to take home those who were left behind".

The actual figures for passengers carried during the first six months show that there was a sharp decline after a very promising beginning, and as events turned out prosperity was not to be the small company's lot. In August the number of passengers amounted to 4,157, followed by 3,800 in September. During October 1,524 passengers were carried but the November and December returns were only 925 and 952 respectively. The financial position of the company was far from secure and the falling off in passenger traffic was a serious threat to the continued existence of the railway. Goods traffic at this time was hardly developed, so there was little revenue from that side of the operations. Nevertheless, the Company remained in business but quickly came to the conclusion that leasing or selling the railway to the neighbouring Lancashire & Yorkshire would be the best way of securing its survival, and to enable this to be done, if such was definitely decided upon, the Company applied for an Act of Parliament, which was passed on 14th August, 1850.

Although people in Liverpool and Southport viewed the building of the railway with satisfaction and optimism, the same could not be said for the residents of the intermediate villages, many of whom considered it a waste of money and a hopeless proposition trafficwise. Indeed, the railway was soon christened the "Shrimpers Line", the carriage of people bent upon this occupation being visualised as the only source of revenue! Little did those pessimists realise what lay in the future. Nobody, not even the most ardent optimists, could have forseen at that early date the vast developments that would be brought about by that little railway along the coast.

The original intention had been to run trains to the Great Howard Street station of the Liverpool & Bury line, but as events turned out the trains of the Southport system never terminated at Great Howard Street because Tithebarn Street (Exchange) station was opened some months before the LC & S line reached Sandhills, at which it connected with the Lancashire & Yorkshire Railway and East Lancashire Railway Joint line into Liverpool (the Liverpool & Bury had become a constituent of the L & Y). It was not until 1st October, 1850 that the company could fully justify its title and run trains into town over the L & Y and E.L. tracks from Sandhills, but on that same day the L & Y took over the working of the Southport line. One of the

20

first acts of the L & Y following this was the introduction of a train service between Southport and Manchester via Sandhills, a most roundabout route to be sure, but there was no direct railway communication between Southport and Cottonopolis at that date, the direct line via Wigan not being opened until 9th April, 1855.

The original Liverpool Exchange station was built to accommodate the three railways. It extended from the East side of Bixteth Street to the West side of Key Street, the latter street being directly opposite Moorfields. Construction commenced in 1849 and involved the clearance of 540 houses and a church. Things moved quickly, and although the contractors did not get possession of the streets until May, 1849, the station and its approach viaducts were completed in only one year. The station was Italianate in design, standing on a platform 30 feet above the streets. Access and egress for vehicles was by means of inclined, curved roadways. There were two iron roofs covering the platforms, one of 136 feet span, the other having a span of 80 feet. The date of opening was Monday, 13th May, 1850.

The original station at Southport was a single platform situated between Eastbank Street and Portland Street. A run-round loop and one siding were provided. In 1850 the station platform was extended right to Eastbank Street and an extra line constructed together with two further sidings on the East side. Under an Act of 5th August, 1850 the railway was extended to a new and more commodious terminal station at Chapel Street, the present Eastbank Street bridge being built concurrently with this extension. Chapel Street station was opened on 22nd August, 1851. In the following year, 1852, the track was doubled between Waterloo and Southport. The only traces of the temporary terminal station surving today are the station house and a small ticket office adjacent to Portland Street level crossing.

Although the Liverpool, Crosby & Southport Railway was operated by the L & Y, the original Company remained in control and at one time proposed to make several diversions of the line but nothing came of this. In 1855 they actually proposed to build a completely independent line from Sandhills into Liverpool, but this was opposed by the Mersey Docks & Harbour Board. It was just a wild dream however, one that never became reality, as there was no money for such a venture. Sale of the line to the L & Y seemed inevitable, but the Company worked the line themselves between 1st January, 1855 and 1st June of that year. A meeting to organise sale to the L & Y was however scheduled to be held in the latter month. The L & Y was not a very efficient railway in those days and many people urged the Southport Company to have nothing to do with it! A letter in the "Liverpool Mercury" of 5th June, 1855 exemplified the feeling:

"So gentlemen, you are about to be swallowed up at last. Long has your doom been sealed; and as a cat amuses itself for a while

with its victim, so you have only been biding your time to be swallowed.

Without a shilling of interest in the line, I warn you that the day will come when you will bitterly repent having sacrificed what might, in a few years, be made one of the best paying lines in the kingdom – a perfect gem of a railway.

Before it is too late, if not so already, let me entreat you before the coming meeting to reconsider the matter, and do not let yourselves be led blindly into a folly so egregious. Insist on an entire change of management – on the adoption of a more liberal policy than has hitherto prevailed – of the encouragement of the local traffic in preference to any other interest; and if a more equitable arrangement cannot be made for the use of the Liverpool terminus, boldly cut at once all connection with the Lancashire and Yorkshire Company, and for a time get your passengers into Liverpool as you best can.

Yours respectfully
H.

Liverpool 30th May, 1855.

As we have already noted, the LC & S Company had obtained powers to allow sale or lease of the railway to the L & Y, and these were finally exercised in June, 1855, when at a meeting held in the Clarendon Rooms, Liverpool on 11th of that month, it was resolved that the line be sold, and this was done three days later. "Herapath's Railway Journal" had editorialised on the position of the Company during the previous month in which they said "This little line of about 17 miles affords a remarkable instance of the insecurity of railway property in England under the English system of Parliamentary Regulation sanctioning unnecessary and competing lines. In 1853 the week's traffic was £325, the corresponding week of 1854 was £491; and the corresponding week of 1855 (the first week of the opening of the Lancashire & Yorkshire and East Lancashire Burscough Branch to Southport) the traffic has fallen to £278. No wonder British Capital is driven to seek investments in the well managed and properly protected railways in foreign countries, where the governments lay down a system of trunk lines".

Although the Liverpool Crosby & Southport Company's line provided the shortest and quickest route between Merseyside and the coastal resort, the East Lancashire provided competition via Ormskirk. Both the L & Y and E.L. companies cut the fares to absurdly low levels to attract traffic, forcing the LC & S company to do likewise, to the detriment of them all. Common sense was eventually restored after loss of revenue caused them to act more wisely.

22

Near the end of its days – Liverpool Exchange station, April 1977.
(Photo: S.G. Jones)

A rare view of Seaforth station taken in 1876 before the line was placed on an embankment. (Photo: J. Ward collection)

A train for Southport at the massive timber Seaforth & Litherland station shortly after the line had been electrified. (Photo: J. Ward collection)

A Liverpool to Southport train approaching Seaforth & Litherland station in September, 1957. The rails formerly used by trains of the by-then closed Liverpool Overhead Railway curve away on the right. This scene has changed drastically in more recent times, only the Up and Down Southport lines remaining whilst the former four-platform station has become a single island platform. (Photo: R. Stephens)

24

A Train Ride of the 1850's

The engineers, locomotive drivers, firemen and operating personel of the early railway have departed this earthly realm long ago, leaving few records of the scenes amid which they worked, in contrast to the huge amount of material concerning civil engineering and locomotive practice which has survived. Indeed, so far as the Liverpool-Southport line is concerned, there are few persons now living who can even remember the end of steam traction, as it is now 81 years since electrification was carried out. However, we will try and recapture the past in describing the sights and sounds of a journey to Southport in the days when the railway was new, an exercise which takes us back to the era of horse-drawn carriages, oil and gas lighting, rough cobbled streets and picturesque fashions. So, turning the calender back to the mid-1850's we shall re-create the scene that met the eyes of a traveller on his way to Southport in those days of long ago.

Ascending the steep flight of stone steps that must be negotiated in order to enter the grand edifice of Tithebarn Street station, with its platforms at the incredible height of 30 feet above the roadway, our traveller enters the concourse and mingles with a mixed crowd of men and women of three distinct social levels — First, Second and Third class passengers. Everyone walks at a sedate pace as, apart from the lack of necessity for hurry, dress modes and manners do not permit of haste if dignity is to be preserved. There is nothing remotely resembling the commuter rushes of the far-distant future when streams of both men and women dash unimpeded by dress or anything else to catch their trains home at the close of the working day. Passengers for Southport obtain their tickets at the appropriate booking office, as each of the three railways serving the station has its own ticket offices and other passenger facilities. At the platform used by the Southport trains a calvacade of short-bodied four-wheeled carriages is drawn up. The roofs of these vehicles are almost flat or may have a slight camber, with the oil lamp holders over each compartment resembling a row of small cylinders standing on end. No provision is made for heating the carriages in the Winter, even footwarmers are futuristic. The First class carriages have comfortable upholstery, much appreciated by the "Merchant Princes" who ride in them. The Second class vehicles are somewhat less luxurious, but the Third class carriages are severely plain, having wooden seats and no ornamentation or aids to comfort of any kind. The Third class vehicles of the 1850's are however, a considerable advance on those of a few years earlier, when people who were forced through poor circumstances to travel Third class rode in open, or at best, vehicles that resembled latter-day cattle trucks — indeed, they were often referred to as wagon passengers.

City gentlemen, neatly attired in beaver hats or toppers, jackets and tight trousers, and with large cravats around their collars recline at ease on the deep cushions of the First class compartments, or are striding along the platform seeking vacant seats. Some carry copies of the headline-less newspapers of the day. The women passengers, dressed á la mode and displaying the latest version of the picturesque but somewhat impracticable crinolene, or hoop-skirt, step along gracefully and with deft manoeuvering of their dress somehow manage to fit themselves and their encircling skirts into the narrow compartments. Cartoons in magazines and newspapers made fun of such fashions as time went on, but they changed very little for years and years.

The less well-to-do passengers, office clerks and shop assistants on their way home from work occupy the Second class compartments, whilst the "artisans, mechanics and daily labourers", to quote the Victorian classfication for those who worked in the factories, building trade, cartage and so on — bewhiskered, bearded and clad in corduroy or fustian — crowd into the Third class carriages, exchanging friendly banter, and smoke their clay pipes, glad to be on the way home after a long day of toil in the manufactures and docks of the busy town and port. Most of them will alight at Bootle or Seaforth, where streets of tiny terraced houses are rapidly spreading over the fields to provide accommodation for the ever increasing numbers of people who are moving into Liverpool and district as the town's expansion proceeds apace.

Up at the head of the train stands the small locomotive, sizzling quietly amid a pleasant aroma of warm lubricant and the tang of smoke. It is a Fairbairn 2-2-2 Tank engine, one of the miscellaneous and motley collection of motive power units of the L & Y system. The bearded driver is making his rounds of the engine with the long-spouted oil pourer, and casting his eyes over the mechanical components in order to make sure the machine is fit for yet another journey. There is little time to rest for enginemen on the Southport line, as they are obliged to struggle along with the mechanically poorest of locomotives discarded from other areas of the system, and these need plenty of looking-after to keep them on the road. The stoker is busy getting the fire in shape for the coming journey, watched by one or two interested passengers who can see the whole process, as there is no cab on the engine to obscure the footplate rituals. A thin haze of smoke drifts from the engine's tall chimney, whilst a wisp of steam hisses through the high-mounted safety valves.

Trains with similar characteristics stand at other platforms and the station is the scene of considerable activity with numerous people, passengers and those who have come to see them off or meet arrivals thronging the platforms with an accompanying bustle of horse-drawn cabs and carts entering or leaving the premises. What an interesting variety of locomotives and rolling stock is present to

26

fascinate the train watcher! Standardisation of equipment is still in the future. Railways are still new and exciting and the staff, underpaid and often overworked as they may be, are proud of their calling and perform their tasks with dignity and care, well aware that they are participants in the greatest travel and transport revolution the world has ever witnessed. Indeed, just up the street from this station, men are hard at work putting together new locomotives at the works of Messrs Bury, Curtiss & Kennedy in nearby Love Lane, one of three engine manufacturers in the district. Railways are opening up hitherto unexplored lands to trade and prosperity, whilst in Britain railway building continues apace, and people fortunate enough to be employed in the new transport mode feel, and are looked upon, as important.

Departure time has arrived for the Southport train and the guard checks that the platform staff have closed all the carriage doors firmly, then, when all is ready blows his whistle and waves his green flag as the signal for "right away ", as guard's will do for a further century or more. The driver, noting that the signals show a clear aspect, pushes over the regulator handle while the stoker winds off the handbrake, and with gentle exhaust-beats and clouds of smoke from the engine's tall chimney, the train gets under way, descending the incline outside the station very carefully and running onto the bridge over the Bath Street branch of the Leeds & Liverpool Canal. The wheels of the locomotive and carriages grunt and screech as their flanges bind on the curved rails at the station approach, and hammer over the points and crossings after which, on gaining plain track they settle into a rythmic clatter over the joints in the short lengths of rail. Numerous barges can be seen on the canal, many of them carrying coal, a function which the railways are now taking over.

Looking backwards towards the just vacated station, the traveller sees the great dome of St. Paul's church in the square which bears the same name — a "Merchant Princes" place of worship destined to lose most of its parishioners as industrial and business premises transform the residential character of the district. Away on the left-hand side, the masts and rigging of sailing ships are ranged along the river frontage whilst tall, gaunt warehouses rear their bulk upwards, some of them being destined to long outlive the sailing ships and be seen by passengers on diesel and electric trains over a hundred years hence!— The carriages bounce and sway as speed increases — the era of smooth rail travel has yet to come with improvements in springling, draw-gear etc., and the replacement of iron rails with steel. Clouds of smoke and steam drift away over the streets to mingle with the outpouring from manufacturing establishments, and at intervals the engine whistle adds its shriek to the medley of sounds that assail the ears in this teeming district.

The first station reached is North Docks, up on the viaduct adjacent to Sandhills Lane, built to serve an ever-expanding district

27

of docks, warehouses and a host of small industries and some large ones too, such as ship repairers and boiler factories. Looking down from the train one sees the streets below thronged with industrial and dockland traffic, with hordes of horses toiling to keep the wheels turning on the dusty setts and cobbles, and the loads moving.

After leaving North Docks station the train crosses the busy Leeds & Liverpool Canal again and soon reaches the junction at which the Southport line diverges from the Preston and Wigan lines, screeching round the curve, passing, on the right a small engine shed, and shortly after passing under Bank Hall Lane Bridge, draws up at the small station of Miller's Bridge, which is immediately on the Liverpool side of that oddly named thoroughfare that passes over the line on a high bridge. Actually the canal bridge gives the station its name. The train is now passing through Bootle, and soon comes to a halt at another small station — Bootle Village, this being on an embankment on the Liverpool side of Merton Road bridge. Both stations just mentioned are destined to be replaced by one — Bootle (Oriel Road), which was opened in 1876.

The Leeds & Liverpool Canal is crossed yet again shortly after the train leaves Bootle Village station and the line continues on an embankment, but descends to road level on the approach to Marsh Lane station which has a level crossing just beyond its platforms. The incline here is the "Achilles Heel" of the railway, for all locomotives have difficulty in surmounting it as 16-carriage trains are being operated, and although these vehicles are four-wheeled and light in weight, the engines are strained on this climb. The train is now passing through a semi-rural area which is destined to become a hive of industry and covered with streets a few years hence. Seaforth station is next reached, where another level crossing takes the road over the railway. There are only a few cottages in the vicinity as yet, and already Liverpool seems far away. People in the fields and lanes watch the trains pass by with interest and curiosity, as the sight is still fairly novel, and every station sees its group of spectators watching arrivals and departures of trains and people.

Beyond Seaforth the railway enters an earthen cutting and curves sharply to reach the small resort of Waterloo — a place that took its name from the famous battle, and after passing over yet another level crossing enters the single platform station which is on the West side of the line. Opposite to the station is a small engine shed. A further level crossing is situated a little distance North of the station at which the railway passes over New Road (later St. John's Road), and yet another level crossing takes Brighton Road over the line.

Beyond Waterloo the railway commences to pass through a district of fields and sand dunes, with some new houses near Crosby. The village has a small station and level crossing, but beyond this place the area is wild and desolate, little development being apparent

28

as yet. The train rolls along the single line at a steady speed, a long trail of smoke drifting away over the fields, carried far by the prevailing South-Westerly wind. There is no other station until Formby is reached, with another level crossing to be passed over before the train enters the platforms. The River Alt too, is crossed, just South of Formby station. Here the track becomes double, a long loop being provided so that two trains can pass each other.

The track reverts to single after leaving Formby, open windswept fields and sand dunes stretching away to the East and West respectively. The driver and stoker on the open engine footplate have a fine job in the Summer, but during the Winter months they are mercilessly exposed to bitingly chill winds, rain and snow along this open stretch of track. Presently Birkdale station is reached and civilisation again, for the men of commerce are having large, comfortable houses built, and the district is beginning to become populous, over 700 people now resident and more coming in as time passes. The day is approaching when Birkdale and Southport will virtually adjoin in a continuous built-up district, mainly due to the ease of travel brought about by the railway.

It is not long now before the train approaches the terminal station at Southport Chapel Street, after passing the now closed temporary station at Eastbank Street and, screeching round the curve, draws up at the platform after a run of 45 minutes duration. Our traveller has reached the end of the line and after alighting watches the locomotive being uncoupled, whence it proceeds to the adjacent shed for servicing. The passengers stream from the platform to waiting cabs and carriages whilst passengers for Liverpool and intermediate stations soon begin to fill the narrow compartments in the never-ending round of coming and going. A fresh engine will take the train out again.

Neat and tidy Waterloo station in early days of the electric train service.
(Photo: Heyday Publishing Co.)

Blundellsands & Crosby station in the early days of the electrification.
(Photo: J. Ward collection)

The Railway in Literature

The Southport line figured in literature once or twice in its early days. For instance, in the year 1853 a satirical little booklet entitled "Lights Along The Line" was written by Henry Grazebrook, who for some reason chose to spell his name backwards in this instance as Yrneh Koorbezarg. The first chapter was a facetious and uncomplimentary commentary on a train journey from Liverpool to Southport, and began with the following somewhat puerile verse:

> *Now Ladies, take your seats!*
> *Show tickets! All right!*
> *Whe-ew! Grunt, grunt!*
> *Snort, snort! Puff, puff!*

The only desirable route from the town of Liverpool to the city of Southport is by rail. This mode of travelling was invented and put in practice by John Bull's younger brother 'Johnathan', who owns a small tract of country on the other side of the herring pond; – this fact is proved by one of brother Johnathan's favourite ballads being entitled 'A Sittin on a Rail'. The country through which the line passes is beautifully disfigured: – for several miles out of Liverpool the heavens are obscured by the graceful wreaths of curling smoke which are vomited forth at intervals from the very bowels of the earth: – this picturesque appearance is only the effect of a great cause. The County of Lancaster abounds in mineral wealth, – that most precious of all diamonds, the black diamond is found in this locality, and as the fusion of this jewel is closely connected with the manufacture of gas, vitriol, soap and other perfumery, extensive edifices are erected for the sole purpose of forming admixtures of various ingredients, to gratify the olfactory nerves and the admiring gaze of thousands at one and the same time, – and as England is a country where everything can be seen and smelt for nothing, no charge is made for the gratification.

The first place we approach is called Bootle, celebrated as a wholesale washing station – myriads of 'the unwashed' from the purlieus of Liverpool, repair to this spot, and at high water boldly advance into the sea, male and female promiscuously, each supplied with a square piece of yellow soap fastened to the right hand by means of a hempen thong and set to work scrubbing themselves and each other in a manner truly gratifying to behold: – the mighty ocean is frequently tinged for miles after one of these operations with mud and soapsuds.

The next place that meets the eye is called Seaforth, only important in being provided with several human menageries, or training establishments for young females, – this village requires no further notice.

We now approach historic ground – Waterloo! – great as the scene of England's greatest battle! Here may the contemplative mind indulge itself in brilliant fancy! – may inflame itself with martial fury! Well may it picture the exciting pageant. Thousands of valiant warriors drawn up in battle array, staring grimly at each other, and polishing their murderous blades in the sand. Each grassy knoll assumes the appearance of a "Mont St. Jean", and the rabbits flying at the grunting of the locomotive forcibly remind the traveller of the flight of the French before the English bayonets – we leave this spot with deep regret.

Further on the spires of Crosby rise from a gentle eminence and the elevated village of High-town is doubtless somewhere near, but quite invisible to the naked eye. It probably floats in the ethereal space where clouds career in majestic grandeur.

To restore the average and adjust the equilibrium, we next find Formby, a calm retreat which lies extremely low; indeed the hamlet might altogether escape observation, but for a Brobdignag bolster reared on end, which acts as a beacon by day and a friendly star by night.

The portion of country we now traverse is remarkable as being the model on which Zahara, or the Great Desert of Africa was formed; Rabbits and windmills are the only animals which can exist in this inhospitable region – the journey, however, now draws to a close, and the traveller's aching eyes fall upon an oasis in the desert: – Southport lies before him.

The geological formation 'along the line' is curious; the lower stratum is coal, the upper was once yellow sandstone (deposited beneath the carboniferous bed during the pre-Adamite period, and recently upheaved by a convulsion of nature) coeval with the 'Lower Silurian' or 'Murchisonian rocks'; but by the action of wind and rain, it has become pulverised, and flies about, the sport of every breeze, and to the extreme annoyance of lady voyagers and third class passengers".

The "Liverpool Mercury" of 29th May, 1849 had an interesting article concerning the journey from Liverpool to Southport, together with information on the resort itself. That part dealing with the railway is as follows:

"A trip to Southport? Easily said; easily done. Ten months have elapsed since we saw the noble village, with its beautiful Broadway unrivalled in any country spot or seaside resort in England. And the drive, outside the omnibus, today, from Dale Street to Waterloo is breezy and refreshing. The atmoshpere is sunny and glowing yet the air is cool enough to be, as the young lady in Yorkshire expressed it, very embracing. The works at the new North Docks, the extraordinary series of arches bearing the Bury Railway, and the junction between the Mersey and his tributary bride from Blackstone Edge, have made gigantic

alterations, where shore and sandhills existed only a few short years ago; and as the space towards Bootle becomes clearer of buildings, the river, the moving vessels, the sea and the Cheshire and Welsh lands attract the eye. Here one can breath and feel thankful for escape from the close and busy streets of (nevertheless) 'the good old town'. The five miles is delightfully run in three quarters of an hour.

At Waterloo station, the present Southern terminus of the Liverpool and Southport Railway, the improvement since last July is striking; the good waiting rooms, the comfortable furniture, the well arranged pay office, are all that could be desired, while the temporary refreshment shed, and the cosy and cheerful purveyor of genuine Eccles cakes and other edibles, gives presage of more perfect arrangements under her care another day. The station so to speak – the platform with its ample shed, well constructed upon well-built walls, is admirable, and worthy of the importance of the line, for important it is destined to be when it is completed to Liverpool. Even here, the uses of the Electric Telegraph are provided for, though it is not likely to exceed a sinecure in point of dignity, unless it should be rendered a cheap substitute for the dreary post. At present letters from Liverpool are trotted round by Warrington to meet the London Down train; then to Newton, Parkside and Wigan, and are carted thence by way of Upholland, and Skelmersdale to Ormskirk whence they are ultimately forwarded to Scarisbrick and Southport, heartily wearied, no doubt, by suffocation in a bag so many hours during a tedious pilgrimage of fifty or sixty miles. Instead of all this, a man might carry the bag to Dale Street in five minutes, deposit it in a locked box under the seat of the driver who would transfer it to a like security at Waterloo, and it would be at the Post Office, Southport in an hour and twenty five minutes from the time it left the hands of Mr. Ranning and his able clerks; the transit would be eighteen miles instead of fifty-six, or, in other words, it would be all the difference between common sense and absurdity which is thus demonstrated to be thirty-eight miles, and would render correspondence between Liverpool and Southport as quick as between Liverpool and London, which at present it is not.

Now we leave the Waterloo station and whisk along the line through a flat, uninteresting country, but we have a companion who knows all the objects around, he points to Sephton and Aughton churches, and the wood which encloses Formby Hall, the old and new Formby lighthouses, the River Alt (which we cross almost imperceptively), and other objects of momentary attention, but the line itself deserves attention, the smoothness and regularity of the action of the wheels gliding along it, no rolling and jolting right and left as upon some undulating rails:

33

and though the line is single, almost throughout, and therefore there is no meeting nor rapid passing of trains generally, yet, near the half-way house (it is sixteen minutes from one and fourteen from the other) there has lately been formed a passing place, at which spot of course, the line is double: a great convenience this for the later trains each day, which can start from the two termini at the same times, with their respective assemblages of evening travellers.

But there is still something better worth notice by a mind attached to progress, namely that in numerous instances, observable along the line, and especially on its Eastern side, patches of cultivation and of abundant produce already showing themselves, where previous to the opening of the railway, not yet a year ago, nothing but neglect and consequent barrenness prevailed around. Food for man and beast may now be seen springing from hitherto waste sandlands and bog, and value reigns where all was valueless before. The railway has brought fertility to the fields within reach of the market. This gives a charm to an otherwise monotonous half-hours ride and realises expectations which many assigned as their reason for siding in the construction of the line. Two blades of grass will now grow where none grew before. Vive, le Chemins de fer!

In three minutes under the half-hour from Waterloo we are at the Southport station: and here again are improvements, the building enlarged, a nice snug waiting room formed and handsomely furnished, and an excellent arrangement made for the safety and convenience of the goods traffic. A side line of railway is brought past the end of the station to the front, where the train waggons can be brought into contact with the waiting carts, and the transfer of goods effected with the greatest facility. This is to be covered in, so as to protect packages from wet weather when it occurs; and it is satisfactory to learn that the goods traffic is so extensive between Liverpool and Southport as to surprise the railway directors who regarded it as of little or no importance in their original calculations, but who have discovered that it is worthy of special and encouraging attention. We have no doubt that it will increase in a remarkable degree, and coupled with the completion of the line to Liverpool, will render the concern as valuable as we always anticipated it would become when it should be completed."

(The remarks concerning the mail seem to have had their effect, for mail was sent via the LC & S Railway from September, 1849).

Hightown station looking towards Liverpool. This photograph, taken in the early days of electric train services, shows the notices instructing passengers where to wait for the various classes of accommodation.

(Photo: J. Ryan collection)

Formby station before rebuilding and construction of the road bridge which replaced the level crossing. View looking towards Liverpool.

(Photo:J. Ward collection)

Freshfield station looking North, circa. 1905. (Photo: J. Ryan collection)

The original station at Ainsdale photographed in L&Y days. This building had been replaced by a smaller timber structure by the time the line was electrified.
(Photo: J. Ward collection)

36

Early Period Train Services

Traffic on the Liverpool-Southport line was extremely sparse in 1848. The first timetable showed only three trains each way (Monday to Saturday) between Waterloo and Southport, as follows:

Waterloo to Southport. 10.15 a.m.; 2.15 p.m.; 5.30 p.m..

Omnibuses in connection left Tithebarn Street, Liverpool at 9.30 a.m., 1.30 p.m. and 4.45 p.m. The 10.15 a.m. train carried First and Second class passengers only; the other two trains carried First, Second and Third class passengers. In the reverse direction trains left Southport for Waterloo at 7.45 a.m., 12.00 p.m. and 3.45 p.m. Omnibus connections were provided for Liverpool. The 7.45 a.m. and 12.00 p.m. trains conveyed First, Second and Third class passengers. The 3.45 p.m. train was First and Second class only. An additional train was run on Mondays and Saturdays only, leaving Southport at 7.15 a.m. The Sunday service consisted of two trains only each way.

During January, 1849 the service was modified. The outward trains from Waterloo on Weekdays were now at 6.10 a.m; 11.00 a.m.; 2.30 p.m. and 6.00 p.m., with connecting omnibuses leaving Tithebarn Street one hour previously. It had probably been found that the three-quarters of an hour allowed for the road journey previously was not sufficient. Actually, the 6.10 a.m. train did not have an omnibus connection. This, together with the 6.00 p.m. train, carried First, Second and Third class passengers, the other two trains conveying First and Second class passengers only.

In the reverse direction trains left Southport at 7.30 a.m. (First, Second and Third class); 9.00 a.m. (First and Second class); 12.00 p.m. (First and Second class); and 4.00 p.m. (First, Second and Third class). Omnibus connections were provided for Liverpool. On Sundays two trains were run between Waterloo and Southport, at 10.00 a.m. and 5.00 p.m. Omnibuses in connection left Liverpool three-quarters of an hour prior to train time — probably the going was easier on Sundays with less traffic on the roads. Between Southport and Waterloo the Sunday trains were at 9.15 a.m. and 4.15 p.m., with omnibus connections from Waterloo to Liverpool.

Upon the extension of the trains to Liverpool, Tithebarn Street, the service was improved. The "Liverpool Mercury" of 1st October, 1850 published the following notice:

LIVERPOOL, CROSBY and SOUTHPORT RAILWAY
Opening to Exchange Station, Liverpool.
The public are respectfully requested to Take Notice that this line will be OPENED FOR TRAFFIC, THIS DAY (Tuesday) the 1st Instant.

37

Trains will run between Liverpool, Waterloo and the intermediate places as nearly as possible every hour.

Contract tickets may be obtained on the 1st and 15th of each month, by application at the Secretary's Office, Sweeting Street, Liverpool.

BY ORDER
R.S. MANSEL
Secretary.

The anticipated hourly service was not realised, but after the extension to Liverpool, the L & Y Company who had undertaken operation of the Southport line made some revisions. On weekdays there were trains from Exchange station to Southport at 7.30 a.m., 10.40 a.m., 12.40 p.m., 4.00 p.m. and 6.00 p.m. In the reverse direction trains left Southport at 7.45 a.m., 9.00 a.m., 12.15 p.m., 3.30 p.m. and 6.15 p.m. There were apparently additional trains between Liverpool and Waterloo, the busiest section of the line. The first train out from Liverpool in the morning carried the mails.

Not only were the trains infrequent, but the first flush of efficiency was not maintained and standards began to fall to the level of those on the rest of the then rather slothful L & Y system. Complaints became vociferous and some were aired in the newspapers. A gem of a letter written by a lady passenger appeared in the "Liverpool Mercury" on 6th April, 1855, as follows:

TO THE DIRECTORS.

"Gentlemen – numerous as have been the complaints in reference to this line, may I be allowed to inquire how it is that the ladies' waiting room at the Waterloo station has lately, by degrees, been dismantled of its furniture, and why it is daily occupied by the porters and attendants on the railway passengers taking their meals; as also making it their retiring room when not actively employed, therefore rendering it inaccessible to those for whom it was intended?

Formerly it was a well furnished, cleanly comfortable little room, with some acceptable books, and much resorted to by the ladies while waiting for the train, to escape the draughts of the platform; but now, if vacated by the present occupants, it is not fit for a lady to enter. There is a dirty, boarded floor, the covering having been removed; the glass is also taken away from the mantlepiece, and altogether it is a neglected spot.

This was not the case when our late Station Master, Mr. Isaac Rigby, had the management; he was an orderly, well-conducted man; and civil and attentive to the humble as well as to the higher classes, and ever at his post of duty.

To the inhabitants, his removal has been a source of great regret, but they have evinced their sympathy with him and their respect for him by presenting him on two different occasions with rather more than £30, subscribed in small sums from large numbers, but with a heartiness and willingness seldom met with, every habitual traveller by the line being anxious to have the opportunity of joining in the compliment to one of the best of Station Masters.

We hear the gentlemen complain that the Tithebarn Street clock, by which they compare their watches, does not regulate the line. Is this intended, should each station have its own particular time, causing constant disappointments?

Hoping for a restitution of our own apartment, I write as one on behalf of the

LADIES OF WATERLOO

26/3/55.

The train services under the auspices of the L & Y both when that company operated the line on behalf of the LC & S and after they had absorbed it, left plenty to be desired. Even after the line had been in operation for over 20 years the train services were the objectives of considerable criticism. The "City Gentlemen", as might have been expected, became increasingly discontented with the prevailing state of affairs, and the Southport line began to figure in "Letters to the Editor" columns of the local newspapers. At the latter end of the year 1870 a body of influential patrons formed a deputation and managed to secure an interview with railway officials, as a result of which they got a slightly better train service. The two following examples of letters to the press are of considerable interest — both appeared in the "Liverpool Courier". The first letter was in the edition of 23rd January, 1871:

TRAINS TO CROSBY.

"Sir. By the time-bills for the present month you will see that the evening trains are made to leave the Exchange station for Waterloo at the respective hours of 8.35, 8.45 and 10.00 p.m. – an interval of an hour and a quarter at that important time of the evening.

For many years there was a stopping train at 9.00 p.m.. The directors, through Southport influence altered this into an express train for Waterloo thus making passengers for the intermediate stations wait until 9.30, which they submitted to with such patience that the directors thought it would bear another strain, so altered the train again to 9.45; and now, as if to try still further the endurance of the public patience, they run no train between 8.45 and 10.00 o'clock.

I suppose their next act of contemptuous indifference to public convenience will be to ask you to give the aid of your powerful influence to oppose the projected tramway to Crosby?"

I am Sir
Your obedient servant
J.C.

The other letter concerned the motive power, as follows:

LIVERPOOL AND SOUTHPORT RAILWAY.

Sir
"Surely the time has arrived when contract holders by this service should protest against such a 'burlesque' upon express travelling as the four so-called 'express' trains really are. The distance between the two termini is just 18½ miles, and the company timetables give 'forty minutes' for the performance of the transit. That such locomotion is by no means express must be readily admitted; but it appears that even this snail's pace cannot be reckoned upon, for during the past week, on two occasions, the engine attached to the 9.00 a.m. train from Southport has broken down from sheer want of motive power, causing a serious delay in the arrival at Liverpool.

It is to be regretted that the deputation which lately waited upon the directors and succeeded in obtaining a more adequate number of trains, did not take the opportunity of pointing out this other material grievance, the more so as it is patent to all who travel on the line that the secret lies in the weakness of the locomotive department. The old stock engines from the main Lancashire and Yorkshire branch are used as long as their boilers will stand any moderate amount of pressure. That such parsimonious economy should be practised in connection with a line which, upon its own traffic, would pay a dividend perhaps second to none in England, is a scandal and a disgrace.

One or two new and powerful engines are wanted, and these must be supplied before anything like justice can be done to the requirements of a very considerable proportion of the whole passengers on this line."

Yours truly
A DISGUSTED CONTRACTOR.

The tramway to Crosby referred to in the first letter did not materialise for many years, and even if it had been built, being horse-operated it would not have offered much in the way of competition to the trains any more than the horse omnibuses did. An electric tramway was however, constructed in the closing years of the nineteenth century by the Liverpool Overhead Railway Company, but this covered only a short distance between two stations on the

Liverpool-Southport line, namely Waterloo and Crosby. Electric trams were of course, quite another proposition to horse-drawn vehicles, and presented a degree of competition, which the railway company nevertheless met, but this belongs to a later stage in the story. The Seaforth Sands terminus of the tramway was some distance from the L & Y station of Seaforth & Litherland, and the same applied at Crosby, where the trams terminated in a residential and shopping area in Crosby village, whilst the station was some distance away down Blundellsands Road. The trams provided a very convenient service so that many people who used the trains instead of the horse-drawn omnibuses deserted the railway between Waterloo and Crosby, although the numbers were small in comparison with the thousands who used the trains on longer trips. The tramway crossed the railway near Waterloo at a spot known locally as the "Five Lamps", named after an ornate lamp standard mounted on an island in the roadway. At Seaforth Sands the Crosby tramway met up with the Liverpool Corporation tramway system which also took some traffic from the railway after conversion from horse to electric traction, but not in sufficient numbers to cause great concern. For longer distances the trains were, and still are, unmatched for speed.

Ainsdale station looking towards Southport in the early days of electric train services. (Photo: J. Ryan collection)

Southport to Liverpool train arriving at Birkdale station, July, 1984. Set No. 508.014 on loan from Wirral lines. (Photo: S.G. Jones)

Birkdale station Up line platform, July, 1984. (Photo: S.G. Jones)

New Trains and a New Image

There is very little available in the way of information concerning the operating practices of such local railways as the Liverpool, Crosby & Southport, and much the same is true of their locomotives and rolling stock. With few exceptions only the larger main line systems have been recorded in any great detail, so that many questions concerning the smaller railways must go unanswered. References to the early railways on Merseyside are extremely scarce, with the exception of the Liverpool & Manchester, which is very well documented indeed as, being the first in the district and the first "Main Line" in the country, attracted widespread interest and attention from professional and lay observer alike. By the time the Southport line was built railways were no longer new and thus taken for granted by a large section of the population.

We have inherited sufficient information to tell us that the Lancashire & Yorkshire Railway was, for many years, widely held to have been one of the worst-managed and most ill-equipped systems in the whole country. Locomotives were underpowered, run-down and subject to mechanical failure. Timekeeping was erratic and the passenger rolling stock decrepit, uncomfortable and uncared-for. The stations, in general, were inadequate in the way of amenities and operational convenience, and the train services poor. Indeed, the railway had become the object of scorn and derision by the end of the 1870's. At length however, the company realised that they had better alter their image or face the prospect of declining business, and thus set about putting their house in order. A gradual and thorough overhaul was carried out and things began to improve to a remarkable degree, and in a fairly short time the L & Y system ceased to be a joke and became a very good railway in most respects, so much so that it ranked highly in public esteem and the bad old days of its youth were quickly forgotten. Train services were improved, large numbers of new locomotives and carriages were built, and the Southport line received its quota of both. The carriages, whilst a considerable improvement over the originals, were still however, fairly austere compared to those on some other railways at the time.

The new generation of L & Y passenger carriages were "six-wheelers", with low-curved roofs, and were severe and gloomy in their appointments. Matching vans for luggage were also introduced. These carriages lasted a very long time in service all over the L & Y system, being retained for branch lines, and main-line excursion traffic, long into the LMS era after the Grouping of 1923. Indeed, a few could still be encountered during the 1960's in use as breakdown train tool vans etc. In the middle 1890's bogie carriages were introduced, and though the riding qualities of the latter were a great improvement over those of the six-wheeled vehicles, they were almost alike so far as construction, appearance and furnishings were concerned. These too, were put to work on the Southport line, and could be found still in use on the LMS system as late as 1947 — indeed some lasted even into the British Railways era, their lives having been prolonged by World War 2, during which every available coach was needed to cope with the demands of traffic.

A well-remembered feature of Lancashire & Yorkshire carriages was the use of horse hair for seat-cushion covering, a most unpopular material so far as passengers were concerned although not to the Company, who found it to be hardwearing and economical. Although decent upholstery appeared in L & Y coaches before 1923, horse-hair seats could still be found in some of the older coaches as late as 1933! After the end of the First World War really comfortable coaches were placed in service, these having eliptical roofs, and wider windows, together with good-riding bogies, but none of them was used on the Southport line due to earlier changes in traction and operation, but back to earlier times for the moment, as we are getting ahead somewhat.

The varied fleet of obsolete locomotives was replaced by new standard designs under the new regime, and so far as the Southport line was concerned this meant Tank engines of the 0-4-4 type designed by Barton-Wright, and later, the ever memorable and splendid 2-4-2 Tank design of J.A.F. Aspinall. The first ten of the latter were sent to the Southport line directly after completion at Horwich works in 1889. Both types performed strenuous and valiant work hauling crowded trains with frequent stops running to exacting schedules, but neither type was ideally suited to dealing with a train service of great frequency demanding quick stops and starts and high acceleration such as the Great Eastern Railway managed with considerable success in the London area with their little six-coupled Tank engines. The L & Y 2-4-2 Tank locomotives were ideal for express and semi-fast trains, and put up some astonishing performances at times — indeed, they served with great distinction over a long period, but were not the answer to the problem of the Liverpool-Southport line upon which the traffic was increasing yearly, so much so that it became ever more difficult to provide adequate train services.

Various ideas were considered by the management including quadrupling of the line. Such work had actually been carried out within the limits of Liverpool and Seaforth, but extension beyond was not favoured due to the huge cost of buying up land, much of it already built over. Another solution had to be found and fortunately, technical progress provided one at the right time. The early years of the present century witnessed the electrification of street tramways, also some railways with problems similar to those of the Southport line, with completely satisfactory results. Here then was the solution, proposed by Mr. J.A.F. Aspinall, the company's General Manager, and this being favourably received by the directors no time was lost in putting it into practice.

Electrification on the "fourth rail" system was decided upon, and the work of equipping the line for electric traction was commenced early in 1903 by the famous Preston electrical manufacturers Dick, Kerr & Company Limited. Such speedy progress was made that on 22nd December of the same year an experimental journey was undertaken with one of the new electric trains. Further trial trips were made, including a run from Southport to Formby on 30th December, 1903. An express run from Liverpool to Southport was made on 20th March, 1904. Two days later, on 22nd March an official "first electric train" left Liverpool Exchange station at 11.35 a.m. From 5th April, 1904 a mixed service of electric and steam trains was operated, followed by a full electric train service which commenced when deliveries of rolling stock had been completed. A setback occured on 11th April, however, when a subsidence at Formby power station forced a return to full steam train services, which continued until 13th May, after which there was no more trouble, and from that day to this the system has worked with great reliability. In the closing days of the steam train service, several of the large 2-6-2 Tank locomotives that were introduced by H.A. Hoy in 1903 were sent to the Southport line but of course, their days were few as they were soon displaced by electrification.

It is of special interest to note that most of the railways that were electrified during the first 20 or so years of the present century were so dealt with in order to win back traffic captured be electric tramways, but this did not apply to the Liverpool-Southport line, which was subjected to little tramway competition. It was steadily increasing business that made electrification a necessity in this particular instance.

Although the decision to electrify the Liverpool-Southport line sounded the death knell of the steam locomotives for regular passenger train services, they were to continue on goods trains, as the Southport line handled a considerable amount of general freight and domestic coal traffic. Neither the 0-4-4 or 2-4-2 Tank engines hitherto employed on the passenger trains suffered any immediate depletion of their ranks, as they were sent elsewhere to work, and many of the latter type were based at either end of the Southport line for very many years afterwards, actually for another half-century! Withdrawal of the 0-4-4 Tank engines commenced during 1908 however, but even so, they were a long time in disappearing, the last ceasing ordinary service in 1921. Incredibly, a few could be found during the 1960's in use as carriage heating boilers at various depots on former L & Y lines, and one which was at Blackpool for many years was moved to Edge Hill and was at work there as late as 1968!

45

The ex-L & Y 2-4-2 Tank engines reappeared on the Southport line 20 years after electrification — on the Southport-London through carriages which they hauled to and from Edge Hill or Lime Street via Bootle Junction, a working which, in company with other former L & Y types they took over from the L & NWR engines after 1921, of which more later.

It was a steam train that made the fastest-ever run on the Liverpool-Southport line. This was a five-coach special operated on 15th July 1899, hauled by one of Aspinall's 4-4-2 "High Flyers", No. 1392, which is reputed to have reached the magical (for those days) speed of 100 miles per hour — a figure open to doubt, but it became legendary and L & Y men were unwilling to disbelieve it! The operation of this express train over a busy line occupied by frequent local trains stopping at all stations must have posed a problem for the traffic Department, but was an exciting spectacle for those lucky enough to have seen the train in full flight with a locomotive of a type which did not normally work over the line.

In order to provide the electric power for traction purposes, a large generating station was built at Formby, by the side of the narrow River Alt, about mid-way between the two termini. Among the equipment installed in this station were 16 Lancashire boilers, four 1500 kw units and one 750 kw unit. These were driven by cross-compound horizontal steam engines. This plant was later increased when further electrification took place. Ashes and clinker from the furnaces were disposed of into wagons running on a narrow gauge railway, whence they were dumped into standard gauge wagons for removal. The River Alt, flowing into the sea nearby, supplied the water for condensing purposes so that it was not necessary to build those great cooling towers which are such a prominent feature of many power stations. Current at 7,500 volts, AC was generated and transformed to 630 volts DC by means of rotary converters. Sub-stations were built at Bank Hall, Seaforth, Birkdale, and at the power station itself. This generating station continued in use until 1946 when obsolescence, coupled with the need for economy brought about its closure. Thereafter current was supplied to the system from the Liverpool Corporation's power station at Clarence Dock.

At first, maintenance and repair of the electric trains was carried out in a small three-road carriage shed at London Street, Southport, which had been converted into a small workshop for the purpose. This soon proved inadequate however, and a spacious new workshop complex was built at Meols Cop in 1913. Constructed in red brickwork and of pleasing aspect, this workshop maintained the electric rolling stock at a high level of efficiency for a period of 57 years. Main overhauls were dealt with at Newton Heath works until that establishment was closed in 1932, the work then being transferred to Horwich locomotive works, which still carries out the

46

overhauls. Meols Cop works, although situated in Southport and absolutely convenient for dealing with the trains (which only had to run a couple of miles under their own power to get to and from the shops) was closed in 1970, and for intermediate overhauls the trains then had to be hauled from Southport to Birkenhead North workshops on the Wirral line via the Bootle Branch, Edge Hill, Warrington, Chester and Bidston, a long, roundabout journey behind a diesel locomotive! Sets were also sent to Reddish, near Manchester for certain attention after closure of Meols Cop works until new extensions of the railway at Liverpool, opened in 1977, provided a shorter route to Birkenhead.

We have moved ahead somewhat, and must return to earlier times. The electrification not only covered the main line from Liverpool to Southport, but was extended to Crossens and formed a short suburban section of the ex-West Lancashire Railway Company's line to Preston. The Crossens line was opened to electric traction on 22nd March, 1904. On 15th February, 1909 the section of the triangular junction between Hawkshead Street Junction and Meols Cop, and the Easterly portion from the latter to Roe Lane Junction were opened to electric trains, which thereafter went to and from Crossens via Meols Cop, reversing at the latter station instead of directly via Hawkshead Street Junction as before, though some peak-hour trains went the former way, avoiding Meols Cop.

In 1906 the section of the North Mersey Branch between Marsh Lane Junction and Aintree was electrified and stations built at Linacre Road and Ford, and later again, in 1914 the live rail was extended from North Mersey Junction to Gladstone Dock. These two sections of line were destined to lose passenger train services in the course of time, of which more later.

The next stage of the electrification programme covered the section of the main line to the North from Sandhills to Ormskirk which was opened to electric trains in stages, as follows: Sandhills to Aintree (19th November, 1906); Aintree to Maghull (1st October, 1909); Maghull to Town Green (3rd July, 1911); Town Green to Ormskirk (1st April, 1913).

By the time the Liverpool-Southport line was electrified, stations had been provided at the following places: Sandhills, Bank Hall, Bootle (Oriel Road), Marsh Lane & Strand Road, Seaforth & Litherland, Waterloo, Blundellsands & Crosby, Hall Road, Hightown, Formby, Freshfield, Ainsdale, Birkdale and Southport. Hillside was added in 1926.

Birkdale signal box with its extended upper floor and abundance of glazing. Once controlling two sets of goods sidings, it deals with passenger trains only nowadays. (Photo: S.G. Jones)

A general view of Southport, Chapel Street station in LMS days.
(Photo: K. Longbottom collection)

Last run of 1939 LMS trains on Saturday, 4 October, 1980. The special train for enthusiasts is seen at Chapel Street station, Southport. A new Class 507 train is at the adjacent platform. (Photo: S.G. Jones)

A train of 1939 LMS rolling stock at Crossens station in 1964, shortly before the Southport-Crossens-Preston line was closed. (Photo: F. Dean)

Rolling Stock Revolution

The electric rolling stock built for use on the Liverpool-Southport service was vastly different to that employed previously. The new cars — they were not referred to as coaches or carriages, were of massive construction, their general design and interior layout following American rather than British practice. The vehicles, built at Horwich and Newton Heath were of the "open" or saloon type with centre aisles and recessed end vestibules fitted with inset doors placed at an angle, which even though they opened outwards, did not project beyond the car side. The first batch of cars had the old style monitor, or what is better known as the clerestory roof. Large fixed side windows were a new and prominent feature so that the cars did not possess that exact American look as did their near contemporaries on the neighbouring Mersey Railway which were pure "USA" in every respect. Four-wheeled bogies were employed, those on the trailer cars being of the standard pattern used on the steam train vehicles, whilst those on the motor units were specially designed for their specific purpose and to accommodate the motors. At first bogies with an 8-foot wheelbase were employed, but were not satisfactory. They were later replaced by 10-foot bogies which gave much better riding qualities.

All the new vehicles had timber bodies on steel underframes, the motor units having sheet steel lining and were thus fireproof. The construction of the bodies followed the American matchboard pattern, and the cars were extremely strong, their good looks being marred only by the very narrow window pillars. Each car was 60 feet in length (later ones being 65 feet long) and 10 feet in width, and thus they were the widest railway vehicles in the country and subject to clearance restrictions when travelling to and from the main workshops on delivery, or when going for their periodic general overhaul.

The First Class cars were provided with upholstered seats, those in the Third Class cars being of varnished cane, and most cars had seats that were reversible in similar fashion to those used in street tramcars.

In similar fashion also to trams and buses, the Third Class cars had bare floorboards, and also a long bar affixed to the ceiling longitudinally, from which strandee straps were suspended. Adequate ventilation was not a particular feature however, as this was provided mainly by box-like vents in the roof decking and by extractors either side of the raised clerestory. The main side windows did not open, though some of these windows were provided with narrow hinged ventilator sections. One or two of the large windows in each car were fitted with hinges so that they could be opened in cases of emergency. In Summer the trains could be stiflingly hot, whilst in Winter draughtiness was a common fault that caused complaints by passengers. At a later date small electric fans were fitted inside the vehicles. A large diagramatic map of the electrified lines was displayed on each bulkhead inside the cars.

The new trains were provided with gangway connections throughout, a feature greatly appreciated by regular passengers who, if they boarded a train at the last minute at either terminal or joined it at an intermediate station, could walk through the cars until they found their own particular group of fellow travellers, or to find a seat should the vehicle they get into be full. The motor units had rather ugly tapering front ends at first, but this form of construction was soon abandoned and a completely flat front substituted due to the fact that the original design subjected the drivers to uncomfortable draughts. Each motor unit was equipped with four 150 horse-power motors — two to each bogie, and weighed 45 tons. A compartment for packages, mails and newspapers etc., was provided. Access to this was by means of a roller shutter on some cars, whilst others were fitted with the more usual sliding doors to the luggage sections. Each motor unit had a destination indicator box on the front at roof level.

A standard electric train consisted of four cars — motor unit + two trailers + motor unit. Five-car trains were formed eventually to deal with the heavy traffic. The original trains were not of the multiple-unit type so it was not possible to couple two sets together and drive from the leading car, but in due course multiple-unit control was provided on some sets and greater flexibility resulted.

Motor units of the multiple-unit trains were fitted with gangways so that in the event of two sets being coupled together, through communication was maintained. Some control trailers had to be provided when MU control was introduced. Later-design cars had dome roofs instead of the clerestory pattern and by the time the fleet was complete a considerable number of detail differences were manifest. There were actually numerous minor dissimilarities to provide interest for the observer.

In the L & Y era the electric trains were finished in a more elaborate version of the standard two-tone brown livery — dark below waist level with light brown above, the car number appearing in the centre flanked by the class designation spelt out fully in gilt characters. Gilt lining was applied to the sides of all vehicles and on the front of each motor unit. The company crest was displayed twice on either side of every car, all this elaboration being in marked contrast to the unembellished livery of the ordinary steam-hauled carriages, but then, enormous pride was engendered by the electrification which was naturally reflected in the fine finish of the rolling stock.

Instead of being fitted with air brakes, a practice on most electric railways, the Lancashire & Yorkshire Company fitted the Southport trains with the standard vacuum brake, a most unusual proceeding because with an intensive service involving fast acceleration and deceleration, the air brake is a better proposition due to it being quicker in action. Nevertheless, the L & Y got along with the vacuum brake apparently without encountering any undue difficulties.

The rapid acceleration from stops, such an important feature of the electric trains, enabled faster schedules to be put into force than was possible with the steam trains using the then existing locomotives, but even had more powerful engines capable of faster acceleration been built, the line was becoming an unsatisfactory proposition for new steam units. The intensive train service, especially on the Liverpool-Crosby section gave little time for engine changing and such operations as replenishing water tanks, fire cleaning, refuelling and the movements necessary to effect these. The changeover to electric traction must have seemed revolutionary to regular passengers, as quite apart from the change of motive power, the magnificence of the new trains of radically different design contrasted vividly with the severely plain carriages of the steam trains, and no doubt the Third Class passengers found the varnished rattan seats a great improvement over stuffed horse-hair cushions which were part of the grim furnishings of the steam-hauled stock. The large picture windows were a new innovation which, besides admitting more daylight, gave an uninterrupted view of the passing scene. It is rather remarkable that there was a reversion to coaches of the compartment type when a new batch of trains was built in subsequent years, which will be referred to later.

In order to operate train services jointly with the Liverpool Overhead Railway over the bridgework of that system, the L & Y provided 12 lightweight cars with multiple-unit control. The prototype car was built by Dick, Kerr & Company in 1905, the rest, which differed in details, following from Newton Heath works in 1906. They were ornately finished but rather antique looking vehicles — even for 1906! "Dingle Cars" was the official title of this rolling stock, but the passengers referred to them as "Orange Boxes" due to their shape and wooden Third Class seating. Each car had a low-curved roof and was provided with controls at each end, because they ran singly during slack periods. The dimensions of the "Dingle Cars" were such that they fitted within the restrictive loading gauge of the Liverpool Overhead Railway. The capacity was 70 passengers per car, with both First and Third class accommodation. The services operated by the "Dingle Cars" were Southport to Dingle, and Aintree to Gladstone Dock via the North Mersey Branch. Both these services were of short duration, as mentioned elsewhere.

After the services for which the "Dingle Cars" were built had ceased, the vehicles were formed into sets of three and worked on the

Ormskirk line for a time, but eventually ended up on the Southport-Crossens line on which they were familiar for many years. The trains always looked rather ancient, especially with the spoked wheels, and were not highly regarded. Once every year, on "Grand National" race day the "Dingle Cars" returned to their old haunts forming "race specials" between Dingle and Aintree via the Liverpool Overhead line. This practice ceased after 1939 due to the war, and by the time racing was resumed the "Dingle Cars" had been withdrawn from service and trains of the LOR system had to be used because the LMS trains, which replaced the old L & Y stock in 1939-1941, could not be run on the Overhead line due to length and weight restrictions.

In the early part of the year 1923, soon after the L & Y had been merged into the London, Midland & Scottish Railway, a special test train was assembled from a set of ex-L & Y steam service compartment type coaches, which were still in L & Y colours. These had the brake vehicles motorised and electrical control equipment installed. This train, which was even fitted with destination indicators, ran for some time on the Liverpool-Ormskirk line, but ultimately vanished and was not seen again. Nothing was published concerning the nature and purpose of the tests which were carried out with this train, but they must have had some bearing on the next chapter of rolling stock development on the electric lines in the Liverpool area. Before coming to this however, there remains to be mentioned three other members of the original fleet. These were the motor luggage vans, later known as baggage cars, which were built for the purpose of conveying traffic that the passenger trains could not handle through the high schedules giving station stops of only 15 seconds duration. Such traffic as mail, fish and newspapers was conveyed in these special vehicles which operated on regular schedules.

The baggage cars (why this Americanism, one wonders?) were single units, which could haul one or two vans if traffic warranted, and they were three in number. The first one was L & Y No. 3028 (later LMS 28497) which was built in 1904. This car had an almost flat roof, and in appearance was somewhat similar to the older passenger brake vans used on the steam train services. The body was of timber, with matchboard sides and a long-wheelbase motored bogie was fitted at one end, whilst a short-wheelbase bogie was fitted at the opposite end. An odd feature was that the motor bogie had spoked wheels whereas the other non-powered bogie had solid disc wheels. This car had a premature end to its busy life, becoming a war casualty on the night of Saturday, 3rd May, 1941 when, together with several other unfortunate coaches it was destroyed in Liverpool Exchange station when the premises were ignited by incendiary bombs and damaged by blast during a heavy air raid.

The second baggage car was L & Y No. 3029 (later LMS 28498), built in 1911. It featured a timber body, clerestory roof, and like its earlier companion had only one bogie motored. This car remained in service until 1952.

The last baggage car added to the L & Y fleet was No. 3066 (later LMS 28499). This was a metal-panelled vehicle with a domed roof, having some affinity in design with the electric stock of the Manchester-Bury rather than the Southport line so far as appearance was concerned. Both bogies were powered on this car, which was built in 1923, entering service after the L & Y had become part of the LMS system. It lasted in service until 1952 and actually received the green livery of British Railways, being the only item of original L & Y Liverpool-Southport electric stock to be painted in this colour. The sequel to the story of the baggage cars belongs to a later part of this resumé.

The years of service coupled with progress in railway carriage design began to tell on the L & Y electric trains by the end of the 1920's, but their end was not yet. During 1927 some new rolling stock was added to the fleet in the form of ten three-coach sets of compartment type vehicles of the kind used by the LMS on local steam train services. Each set consisted of a motor brake-third, trailer composite and driving trailer brake-third. The motor units weighed 56 tons, the other two types weighing 28 tons each. Each motor unit was equipped with four 265 horse-power motors by Metropolitan Vickers. The vehicles forming these trains were built as follows: Motor units by the Metropolitan Railway Carriage & Wagon Company, Smethwick; trailers by Clayton Wagons Ltd., Lincoln; driving trailers by the Midland Railway Carriage & Wagon Company, Birmingham. The trains were known to the staff as "Lindberghs" because they were introduced in the year that Colonel Lindbergh flew the Atlantic Ocean in the monoplane named "Spirit of St. Louis".

The doors of the compartments on the 1927 trains were very heavy, the timber bodies being metal sheathed. Bars across the droplights prevented passengers from leaning out. Similar trains were built for the London (Euston)-Watford services, and later, in 1931 for the newly electrified Manchester South Junction & Altrincham Railway. As a matter of fact five Liverpool area trailer coaches were transferred to the MSJ & A line in 1940.

The use of the compartment type trains was almost always confined to the Liverpool-Ormskirk and Liverpool-Aintree services, and the only time a Southport line passenger got a ride in one was when the train was used for service on that line when on its way to or from Meols Cop works for repairs, but the occasions were very rare.

The 1927 trains were very fast, but gave a rough and noisy ride when getting near time for overhaul. They were extremely popular when they were introduced, but declined in public esteem after 1939 when another lot of new trains began to displace the old L & Y stalwarts. Even so, the compartment type trains still had some supporters who liked the semi-privacy in comparison with the "open" arrangement of the L & Y cars. Time eventually caught up with the compartment stock and the trains were removed from service during 1962, thereafter languishing in sidings at Meols Cop for some time for possible further use at busy holiday times or Aintree race traffic, but they did not however, see any more service and were broken up during 1963. They were not replaced by new rolling stock due to the fact that the economy axe was being wielded over the Southport and Ormskirk lines during 1962-63; the simple expedient adopted was the re-casting of the train service so that they could be done without!

To return now to the subject of the baggage cars. These were replaced when out of use for repairs by Ormskirk line compartment coaches running either singly or in pairs, with the merchandise piled up on the seats in the compartments. After Nationalisation it was possible for some months to see a coach in LMS red coupled to one in BR green livery, one being lettered LMS, the other carrying the title BRITISH RAILWAYS. In 1952 however, two Ormskirk line coaches, motor unit No. 28300 and driving trailer No. 29106 were properly rebuilt as baggage cars at Derby works, and numbered M28496 and M28497 respectively. They were sometimes supplemented by compartment coaches borrowed from passenger service however. These two cars were in constant use until 1965 when the service was done away with, then they lay idle until June 1966, when they were stripped of collector shoes and control gear and hauled to a scrap metal yard at Stanley, Liverpool, on the Bootle Branch, and broken up after languishing there for several months. Both cars were in very good external condition when withdrawn, the green paintwork being clean and unscarred.

In 1964 a baggage car of Southern Region design appeared on the Southport line. This vehicle, No. E68000 was built at Eastleigh in 1955 for the Tyneside electric lines, but became redundant when conversion of those lines to diesel train operation took place. This lone vehicle of its type seems to have done little work on Merseyside and was stored at Meols Cop for some time, being broken up in March, 1967, after a short life, as there was nowhere else where it could be employed.

The running of the baggage cars was one of the more interesting facets of the Southport line operations. The vehicles always excited interest among the passengers, especially when an expectant crowd waiting on a station platform, noting the signal arm move to all-clear and expecting their own train to arrive, would see instead the single unit roll into the station, and if no porter was out waiting for it, the driver would give a toot on the whistle to announce the arrival of the car. It would stop for boxes of fish to be unloaded for delivery to local fish and chip shops, or parcels, or to pick up or set down items for delivery to, or from, distant stations. Newspapers were also carried and unloaded at all stations both morning and evening. When the car arrived at Liverpool Exchange or Southport, porters and postmen would busy themselves with loading or unloading. Now alas, this service has gone, another step in the decline of the railways' role in the local transport scheme.

By the mid-1930's, in common with their near contemporaries on the neighbouring Mersey Railway, the L & Y eletric trains were sometimes the subject of "Letters to the Editor" of local newspapers, occasionally complimentary but more often derisory, demands for their replacement being frequently made. Still reliable in service their motors were however obsolete and becoming noisy, their old control gear making for jerky starts, their varnished cane seating gave spartan comfort by the standards of the late 1930's, and the timber bodies expensive to maintain. However, one day in August, 1939, the last month of peace before Europe was plunged into conflict, a steam locomotive made its way from Derby to Southport hauling a set of bright new red-liveried electric cars with a goods brake van either end, thus the days of the old L & Y trains became definitely numbered, because this was the first to arrive of a complete new fleet of trains, most of which were delivered over a period of little more than two years.

The new fleet consisted of 34 three-car and 25 two-car trains, of all-steel construction, built in the LMS works at Derby. These trains, minus collector-shoe gear were hauled to Southport by steam locomotives, and gained the Southport line via Olive Mount Junction, passing over the ex-L & NWR Bootle Branch and onto the electric line at Bootle Junction, proceeding thence to Meols Cop works via Southport South Junction. Locomotives employed on delivering the new units were the Stanier 2-6-0's, Class 4F 0-6-0's and Stanier Class 5 4-6-0's. It took about eighteen months to complete the rolling stock change, so for a while old and new trains operated the services together, but the former dwindled away gradually, withdrawn sets being hauled away to Horwich, from which there was no return.

The LMS trains of 1939 (which for the most part were still going strong in the late 1970's and therefore among the oldest trains in BR service) were generally similar to London Underground trains in their design and interior arrangement, and were of smaller dimensions than the L & Y trains which they replaced. The saloon, or open type interior of each car included transverse seating arranged in groups, back to back, with two or three persons aside, and longitudinal seats adjacent to the automatic sliding doors, of which there were two sets either side of each car. There was no gangway connection between the cars making up a set, a feature that the old trains possessed — its absence was considered a drawback by regular passengers, and the new trains took some getting used to in this respect.

The new rolling stock consisted of 59 Third class motor, 34 driving trailer Composite and 59 trailer cars. Nine of the latter were Composite, First/Third initially, but were altered to Third class only shortly after World War 2. The motor units weighed 40½ tons, each having two four-wheeled bogies equipped with Timken roller bearings and four 230 horse-power motors. Control equipment and motors were supplied by The English Electric Company. Construction of the trains was carried out on the most advanced lines for the time, the most notable feature being the tubular girder design of the car bodies, which was achieved by welding the floor, sides and roof in one piece. Each car was 66 feet, 6 inches in length by 9 feet wide. Electro-pneumatic braking and door gear were incorporated, the doors being operated by the guard with push-button control. Very little luggage space was provided in contrast to the old trains which had a spacious compartment for miscellaneous traffic. The maximum speed of the LMS trains was 70 miles per hour, and even when approaching the 40-year mark of continuous service the trains were still masters of their work and swept along effortlessly carrying the crowds on business and pleasure with wonderful reliability, so much so that a train failure on the Southport line was a rare event. In old age their work became more strenuous when the Link line with its steep incline was opened in 1977.

By the end of 1941, despite war conditions, including air raids most of the new train sets had entered service and the L & Y trains had almost completely vanished. Some individual L & Y cars were, however, retained for such duties as temporary mess rooms, mobile stores etc., most of them shorn of their running gear except for those likely to be moved from time to time. One car (No. 29331) still on wheels was parked in Freshfield goods yard for a time, and two others, "grounded" at Southport alongside the locomotive shed survived until 1950. At least one six-car train was held as a reserve however, until the air raids were safely past, and on the cold, snowy night of Monday 26th January, 1942 this train, like a ghost from the past, rolled into Liverpool Exchange station causing quite an amount of interest among regular passengers who believed that all the old trains had gone! Another former L & Y motor unit was used as a baggage car well into the war period.

In comparison with the aged L & Y trains, the new ones, with their comfortable upholstery and modern decor were quite luxurious, though a minor irritation was the incessant vibration of the sliding window vents in the motor units which was particularly noticeable when the train was accelerating, a trouble which could have been remedied with rubber packing. These trains were destined to perform 40 years of service!

57

Sundry items of interest remaining to be mentioned in connection with the 1939 trains concerns firstly that as new, some of the motors and driving trailers had a metal visor above the front look-out windows, but this fitting was subsequently removed. All trains had a form of "chime" whistle originally, but British Railways replaced these with the standard horn as used on the diesel trains.

In October, 1977 two three-car sets of new British Rail standard Class 313 electric rolling stock were given trials on Merseyside. They were from Hornsey depot on the London, King's Cross-Northern suburban lines, and were equipped with both collector shoes and pantographs. The trains were hauled up to Allerton traction maintenance depot, then taken to Hall Road depot via Edge Hill and the Bootle Branch. Passengers noted them with considerable interest because by this time the provision of new trains had become an urgent necessity, but these two were not for use on the Southport line, they were merely on trial to establish the requirements for new stock in the way of clearances and the disposition of collector shoe gear and other fundamentals. The trains stayed for a couple of weeks and were then sent back to London. They were, however, the precursors of a new fleet already on order for Merseyside lines. The first two sets for Merseyside use arrived at Hall Road depot in August, 1978.

The new trains, built at York B.R. works, were the first members of Class 507, a new standard design for suburban service. The three-car sets are composed of driving motor + trailer + driving motor. The powered cars have four G.E.C. 110 h.p. traction motors, the trains being capable of reaching a maximum speed of 75 miles per hour. Automatic couplings are fitted, whilst through communication is provided throughout the train (as on the old L & Y sets). Second class accommodation only is provided, of the "open" saloon type with three and two back-to-back seating. A three-car set seats 232 passengers, as compared with 268 in the displaced ex-LMS trains, although there is ample standing toom for rush-hour crowds. Telephonic communication is provided between driver and guard, and a public-address system allows the train crew to make announcements to the passengers. A detracting feature of the new trains however is the smaller number of windows, some seats being so placed that looking out is difficult. Nevertheless, the trains are comfortable and air-suspension makes for a smooth and quiet ride. The cars are 9ft 3 inches wide.

Trial runs and driver training journeys were performed by the first two class 507 units, while one was used for the official opening of the Merseyrail inderground system which was performed by H.M. The Queen on Wednesday 25th October, 1978. The first set to enter public service (507 002) made a ceremonial run from Ormskirk to Liverpool on 1st November, 1978, carrying fare-paying passengers, thereafter the two units ran daily. Further sets began to arrive during 1979 and as they did so, ex-LMS sets were withdrawn and hauled away for scrapping. Many old sets were parked out in the Wirral, at Shotwick sidings, but were later moved to Crewe South, languishing at the latter place for many months, thence going to Norwich, Snailwell and Rotherham for breaking up.

Even while the ex-LMS sets were being withdrawn, shortages of rolling stock persisted due to the additional services being operated, coupled with intermittent failures of both old and new trains, so several sets of Wirral section rolling stock were transferred to the Liverpool lines and used mainly on the Garston-Kirkby service. Even when all the class 507 units had been received, four three-car Wirral sets remained, based at the new Kirkdale depot and were still in use well in to 1982. They returned home after initial problems with the new trains had been resolved and they had become more familiar to the staff.

A number of ex-LMS sets were retained for peak-hour services until September, 1980 when they were withdrawn en masse, and spent their last days parked at Kirkdale, Hall Road and Southport. They did not finish their days unsung however, for it was felt in official circles that rolling stock which had given 40 years of magnificent and largely trouble-free service deserved a memorable send off, and to the great delight of those who had an affection for the old trains, a special rail tour was arranged on Saturday, 4th October, 1980, advertised as the last public journey of a class 502 electric train.

No ex-LMS trains had run for several weeks, so the appearance of the six-car special train at Liverpool Central on that memorable day caused considerable excitement. About 200 people (mostly male) availed themselves of the opportunity to make the trip. The train ran to Garston, thence to Kirkby, passing through Central non-stop, being the first passenger-carrying train to do so, to the wonderment of people waiting on the platform. From Kirkby the train proceeded to Sandhills and reversed in the reversing siding, again the first train with passengers aboard to do this. A fast run was then made to Southport, at which there was a break of two hours, to enable a visit to the nearby transport museum (Steamport) to be made. Inside the museum were a motor and driving trailer of the "Southport" stock, preserved from scrapping, a fact noted with great satisfaction. The next stage of the journey was back to Sandhills, reversal again, and on to Ormskirk, at which there was a halt of 10 minutes, after which the final part of the trip was made to Liverpool Central, at which everyone reluctantly alighted. The train next departed for Kirkdale, and ultimate scrap.

As it happened the ex-LMS trains did not entirely vanish, because two 2-car units were retained for de-icing duties during the Winter months. Each unit consisted of a motor and driving trailer fitted with tanks for the anti-freeze liquid plus the equipment for dispensing it. One train was kept at Hall Road or Kirkdale, the other being based at

Southport. Later however, some new class 507 trains were fitted with de-icing gear rendering the ex-LMS trains redundant. Trouble with the new trains losing adhesion in the "wet leaves" season led to the equipping of a three-car Wirral train with apparatus for sanding the rails — known as the Sandtite train, which sees service mainly during the Autumn when trees shed their leaves and, landing and sticking to the rails, causes wheels to slip and also affects braking. By October, 1980 a total of 33 class 507 sets were in service.

The two-car ex-LMS train preserved at "Steamport" in Southport belongs to the National Railway Museum, and during the Winter of 1983-84 was restored to its LMS condition and is to be repainted in the red livery of that former system. It is a pity that a trailer car was not preserved also, to make a three-car set, as only for a short time did two-car trains operate, and then only on the Ormskirk service. Nevertheless, it is good to know that these two ex-LMS vehicles are safely preserved.

Before leaving the subject of rolling stock, it is of interest to recall the unusual arrangement for dealing with the Aintree race traffic in the earlier days of electric traction. The L & Y Company retained several sets of ancient six-wheeled gas-lit compartment carriages, ten per set, permanently coupled, and these were sandwiched in between two electric motor units making a useful high-capacity train to shuttle to and fro between Liverpool Exchange station and Aintree. As the electric vehicles were much higher and wider than the old steam stock, these trains presented a distinctly odd appearance. The two electric cars were Third class, but on race days became First class, temporarily, the Third class passengers rode in the six-wheelers! The cables for the control gear passed along the roofs of the old carraiges. The use of these special trains was continued into LMS days, but the six-wheeled carriages were replaced by bogie stock from the former L & Y and Midland systems. The practice was discontinued in the early 1930's and ordinary electric train sets used instead of the "specials".

Early in the present century a then novel way of capturing traffic from outlying districts not served by the railway was the use of motor buses as feeders to the trains, and in 1907 the L & Y Company introduced a bus service between Crosby station and Thornton. This proved to be unremunerative however, and was subsequently abandoned. The idea has been resumed more recently in a big way with feeder bus services connecting with trains at Waterloo, Formby, Ainsdale and other stations on the Merseyrail system.

Aintree station looking North, in late L&Y days. Gas lamps still illuminate the platforms through which pass electrified rails. (Photo: J. Ryan collection)

Looking North from Aintree station in the Summer of 1956. Two sets of 1927 compartment-type trains are standing in sidings, and a fine array of signals give a busy air to the scene. Today most of this track has gone, and there are no signals. (Photo: R. Stephens)

Maghull station looking North on a Winter day, February 1985.
(Photo: S.G. Jones)

Maghull signal box and level crossing, July 1984. View looking towards Liverpool. Pedestrians wait for the barriers to lift after passage of a train.
(Photo: S.G. Jones)

More Traffic — More Trains

The relatively poor service provided on the Liverpool-Southport line in its early days was perhaps justified in view of the sparsity of population, but was gradually improved, though not sufficiently so for many years. Development of the residential areas eventually forced the management to increase the services and from the original five trains each way daily in 1848 the service, by 1863, consisted of nine trains in each direction on weekdays between Liverpool and Southport, and about 34 local trains each way between Liverpool and Crosby. On Sundays four through trains were run in each direction and six locals between Liverpool and Crosby. By the 1880's there were about 18 through trains in each direction between Liverpool and Southport and 30 or so locals between Liverpool and Crosby. By 1903, the last year of full steam operation there were approximately 36 through trains each way and a similar number of locals as far as Crosby, on weekdays. On Sundays nine through trains were provided in each direction and four between Liverpool and Crosby, also four between Southport and Crosby. The vast majority of trains called at all stations but a few expresses, calling only at Birkdale were run for business people in the morning and evening peak periods. The expresses made the trip in 25 minutes, and this amount of time was also taken by the Liverpool-Crosby trains, with seven stops. Through stopping trains between Liverpool and Southport required 54 minutes for the $18\frac{1}{2}$-mile journey.

When full electric working was put into force the number of weekday trains was considerably increased. The through service now consisted of approximately 50 trains each way, calling at all stations, with about 56 more trains on the local service between Liverpool and Hall Road, the latter station having replaced Crosby as the terminus for local trains. There were also about a dozen express trains calling only at Birkdale. On Sundays 34 trains were provided in each direction, all being through trains, no locals between Liverpool and Hall Road being provided as was the case on weekdays. This excellent service was continued for many years but the expresses were gradually dropped out of the schedules, these being replaced by semi-fast trains stopping at about half of the intermediate stations in order to meet the needs of a great number of passengers, due to the development of the residential districts.

As an example of the intensive rush-period train service into and out of Liverpool Exchange, this time-table of 1928 shows how well the LMS Company catered for local passengers on the Southport line. These were in addition to Ormskirk line trains and steam trains to and from places further afield — all operated with manually worked semaphore signals and points, no electronic signals or computers then!

Arrivals at Liverpool Exchange. Morning peak-period:

8.40 a.m.	Southport, Birkdale, Formby, Hightown and Sandhills only.
8.43 a.m.	Stations from Hall Road.
8.46 a.m.	Stations Southport to Formby, Blundellsands & Crosby.
8.48 a.m.	Stations from Hall Road.
8.52 a.m.	Aintree via Marsh Lane.
8.55 a.m.	Stations from Hall Road.
8.57 a.m.	Southport, Birkdale and Freshfield only.
9.00 a.m.	Stations from Southport.
9.05 a.m.	Stations from Hall Road, except Bootle and Bank Hall.
9.10 a.m.	Stations from Waterloo only.
9.13 a.m.	Southport, Birkdale, Ainsdale and Sandhills only.
9.16 a.m.	Stations from Southport.
9.18 a.m.	Blundellsands & Crosby, Waterloo and Seaforth only.
9.25 a.m.	Stations from Hall Road.
9.30 a.m.	Stations from Southport.
9.34 a.m.	Southport, Birkdale, Ainsdale, Formby and Hightown only.
9.38 a.m.	Stations from Hall Road.
9.46 a.m.	Stations from Hall Road.
9.51 a.m.	Stations from Southport.
9.54 a.m.	Southport, Ainsdale and Freshfield only.
9.58 a.m.	Aintree via Marsh Lane.
10.04 a.m.	Stations from Hall Road.
10.11 a.m.	Stations from Southport.
10.14 a.m.	Southport, Ainsdale and Freshfields only.

Normal service after this arrival.

A correspondingly intensive service operated in the evenings, with 29 trains departing from Exchange for Southport line stations between 4.32 p.m. and 6.28 p.m. On Saturdays the peak-period was mid-day, with 28 trains departing between 12.17 p.m. and 2.32 p.m.

Running times for the electric trains in L & Y days were as follows: all-stations trains between Liverpool and Southport, 34 minutes; local trains between Liverpool and Hall Road, 17 minutes; express trains 25 minutes, the latter being the same as the former steam train schedule.

In the year 1939 stopping trains were taking 40 minutes for the through journey — an increase of six minutes on the original electric schedule. The war years saw little change except for enormously increased traffic, but it had been the policy to gradually decrease the number of local trains between Liverpool and Hall Road. The service pattern continued almost unchanged after Nationalisation in 1948. In 1960 there were approximately 68 through trains in each direction on weekdays, certain peak-hour trains running non-stop as far as

Waterloo, Crosby, Hightown or Freshfield, with a few local trains terminating at Hall Road. The economies which were applied from 1962 were to take increasing effect, so much so that history began to repeat iself — complaints regarding the train service began to be heard again! Even with the cuts however, the service was still an excellent one but the writing was ominously on the wall at that time — the "Beeching Plan" was about to be published.

The train service at the beginning of 1966 consisted of about 54 each way between Liverpool and Southport, calling at all stations, three semi-fast trains running non-stop between Liverpool and Waterloo in the evening rush period, and five peak-time locals between Liverpool and Hall Road. In the opposite direction two semi-fast trains were run between Southport and Liverpool calling at all stations to Waterloo, thence non-stop to Liverpool, one train from Southport to Formby thence non-stop to Liverpool, another which called at all stations to Hightown thence non-stop, and one serving all stations to Hall Road, continuing non-stop for the remainder of the journey. There were also a number of stopping trains between Hall Road and Liverpool It will be seen that in the main, the Liverpool-Southport service remained much as it was in L & Y days until about 1960, the service between Liverpool and Hall Road having virtually vanished. It is on this section that competition from buses has been most intense, and of course, the enormous increase in car ownership has taken its toll.

The service was whittled at during April, 1966 with the withdrawal of 27 trains including some early morning and late night trains, whilst further economies were put in force during the Winter of 1968, when the Sunday train service on the Southport line was made hourly between 8.00 a.m. and 11.00 p.m. This was to be the pattern for several years afterwards, though the frequency was doubled on Summer period Sundays. In 1968 too, the running of train services on Christmas Day and Boxing Day ceased.

It seemed as though the Liverpool-Southport line was sliding downhill in the late 1960's but a great awakening was actually taking place in the realm of public transport and it was beginning to be realised in official circles that rail transport was the answer to traffic problems in large cities and conurbations — something well known and acted upon on the European Continent and elsewhere for years. The formation of Regional Transport Boards in 1969 brought Merseyside transport under control of the Merseyside Passenger Transport Authority, which became responsible for local bus, ferry and train services, and one of this bodies' first acts was to breath a new spirit into the Liverpool-Southport line by introducing a 15-minute train service all day on weekdays and Summer Sundays — not so easy to maintain however, as a proportion of the rolling stock had been scrapped. The Winter period Sunday service provided a train each way every 30 minutes. Running time for all-stations trains in 1972 was 40 minutes, a little slower than in L & Y days, but there is an additional station to be called at, namely Hillside which did not exist when the line was first electrified. In 1984 the running time was 37 minutes (from Moorfields, which corresponds with the former Exchange station). In 1975 an hourly express service was introduced, but did not last for long.

In spite of all that has happened to the Liverpool-Southport train service in recent times, it is still frequent and regular, and nobody has long to wait for a train. A policy of closing certain stations on Winter Sundays was put into practice in 1976 and continues, with a reduction of the train service to one every 45 minutes, but when the Link Line was opened in May, 1977 revised and more frequent services were introduced. The Sunday service was now a train every half-hour. In Summer a 15-minute Sunday service was provided.

Before leaving the subject of train services there remains to be mentioned two very useful facilities now gone, namely through carriage services between Southport and London (Euston) via Liverpool, and through carriages between Birkdale and Manchester (Victoria).

The London service commenced on 1st May, 1886 upon the opening of a connection between the L & NWR Edge Hill-Alexandra Dock line at what became known as Bootle Junction. Four trains in each direction were provided, worked by L & NWR locomotives. Regular calls were made at Seaforth, Waterloo and Birkdale, but conditional stops were made at certain other stations on notice being given to the stationmaster by outward passengers, or in the reverse direction to the guard of the train in the case of passengers wishing to alight (only passengers from North Wales or South of Crewe could request the train to stop).

By 1910 the trains were making regular stops at Seaforth, Waterloo, Crosby, Formby and Birkdale. Passengers from London for Hightown and Altcar could be set down on notice to the guard. The service continued well into World War I (reduced to three trains however), but in 1917 it was suspended, along with many other train services in that grim year. The service re-commenced in 1920, between Southport and Liverpool, Lime Street or Edge Hill (no through carriages being provided), but these were resumed in 1921 however, worked by L & Y locomotives instead of L & NWR as previously. Types used were Barton-Wright and Aspinall 4-4-0's, 0-6-0 goods, 2-4-2 Tank and sometimes a "Dreadnought" 4-6-0. The through carriages were attached to a London train at Lime Street, whilst on the Northbound journey they were detached at Edge Hill and worked onwards to Southport by an engine which waited in the bay platform (known as "Southport Bay"). Four trains each way were provided, as in pre-war years.

Upon the commencement of the second World War on 3rd September, 1939, the service was suspended, but in January, 1940 one train each way was reinstated. This worked well until the blitzkrieg when the train was likely to be caught up in air raids in both Liverpool and London and sometimes ran hours late, or did not get through at all. Due to these difficulties, the service was suspended from 2nd May, 1941 (in the worst week of Liverpool's air raids) and was not reinstated until 7th October, 1946, but only one train each way. It was not until 27th September, 1948 that the old service of four trains in each direction could again be provided, although it was reduced to two trains each way during the winter months. This pattern prevailed until the provision of through electric train services between Liverpool and London which commenced on 18th April, 1966.

The last through carriage working from London to Southport took place on Friday, 15th April, 1966. The coaches were detached from the main-line train at Edge Hill at 9.20 p.m., and strengthened by extra vehicles for railway enthusiasts and for a party of members of the Railway Correspondence and Travel Society, set off for Southport at 9.51 p.m. The engine on this occasion, specially requested, was class 5 4-6-0 No. 45156 "Ayshire Yeomanry", one of the very few of this class to carry a name. It had spent most of its career in Scotland but was stationed at Southport at this time.

Initially it was proposed by BR to discontinue not only the through carriage service but to provide no connection at all between Southport line services and those to and from London, not even a bus service between Lime Street and Exchange stations, but fortunately such did not happen. Instead of through carriages, which apparently could not be tolerated on a modern, highly standardised railway, a service of 2-car DMU trains was instituted between Southport and Liverpool (Lime Street). It was hoped that shoppers would use this service as well as London passengers, but owing to a shortage of diesel units, only two trains in each direction could be provided at first. This service commenced on 18th April, 1966 and ran Mondays to Fridays — it did not operate on Saturdays until 18th June.

In 1967 a much improved service commenced, running on Saturdays as well as weekdays with one or two exceptions. Not all trains called at every station along the Southport line — some stations were omitted by certain trains. About eight trains in each direction were provided and this service continued until the opening of the Liverpool Link Line in 1977, of which more later.

It was only during the Summer months that the Lime Street-Southport trains carried full loads. There was very little advertising for the service in the beginning and virtually none in its latter days, its existence not being generally known except among railway employees and enthusiasts who spread the word when opportunity offered. Many enthusiasts travelled the Lime Street route for its unusual interest. Sometimes passengers bound for Liverpool from stations between Southport and Bootle boarded a diesel train (it is surprising how unobservant many people are) and were astonished at finding themselves persuing a course round the outskirts of Liverpool and ending up at Lime Street instead of Exchange station! At its worst, it was a hit-or-miss operation, initial enthusiasm having died, not even being included in the public timetables latterly. Sometimes, due to train failure, a bus was provided to cover the service. It finally ceased when the Loop Line underground station at Lime Street was opened on 10th October, 1977, although passengers from Southport had to change at Moorfields or go through to Central station and walk across to Lime Street.

The Birkdale-Manchester through carriages were provided primarily for businessmen, and were hauled to St. Lukes by a steam locomotive and attached to a Southport-Manchester train on the outward morning journey, the reverse of this operation taking place on the evening return journey. Only one service each way daily was provided. Normally passengers from Birkdale to and from Manchester changed trains at Southport Chapel Street (and still do so today). The through service was abolished many years ago.

Town Green station, looking North, July, 1984. The original station building happily still survives.   (Photo: S.G. Jones)

The simple "halt" station at Aughton Park, opened in May, 1907. Platforms and shelter accommodation were built when the line was electrified in 1913.
(Photo: J. Ryan collection)

Liverpool-Ormskirk train (set 507.027) entering Aughton Park station, July, 1984. The ugly modern lamp standards marr an otherwise picturesque scene.
(Photo: S.G. Jones)

From Sombre Brown to Rail Blue

The livery of the electric trains has changed along with the successive changes of ownership. The two-tone brown of the Lancashire & Yorkshire Railway survived until the Grouping of 1923, though it was some considerable time after that date before all the trains had been repainted in the red livery of the newly formed London, Midland & Scottish Railway. When the L & Y and L & NW companies joined forces in 1922 some of the electric cars were lettered L & NWR, and one or two even carried the latter company's crest. The LMS livery was actually crimson lake, the so-called "Midland Red", which was continued up to Nationalisation in 1948, and again, it was some time after this event before all the trains had been repainted in British Railways livery.

A minor change with the introduction of the new trains in 1939 was the practice of showing the fleet number on the front of each motor and driving trailer unit, and this was also applied to the Ormskirk line compartment sets. From 1942 coach ends were painted black, with the exception of the control ends of motor and driving trailer units.

Upon Nationalisation the livery chosen for electric multiple-unit trains was malachite green with straw coloured lining. First Class cars were designated by a large figure 1 on the doors. The vehicles were lettered BRITISH RAILWAYS in full at first, until the famous Lion and Wheel emblem had been designed, and this was applied instead of the title, and was followed in 1956 by the more elaborate and dignified BR crest. Only motor units acquired the crest however. About 1956 the livery was changed to dark green without any lining, First class accommodation being indicated by a straw-coloured stripe below the roofline. Yellow squares were next applied to train ends to act as a warning to men at work on the track by making the trains more easily visible. This was followed by painting in yellow of the full width of the car up to the level of the look-out windows.

When British Railways became BRITISH RAIL in connection with what was termed the new corporate image, during 1966, the colour of the trains was changed to all-over "rail blue", with the double arrow symbol in place of the former crest applied to motor and driving trailer units only. The first Southport line set to appear in this livery made its debut in March, 1968. In contrast to previous practice, the yellow paint was applied to full height on the end of each train set and carried round the side for a few inches. Just as trains composed of LMS red and BR green vehicles could be seen for some years after Nationalisation, so green and blue sets often worked coupled together, and it was not until early in 1972 that repainting of the trains was completed. The bright vermilion, universally applied to buffer beams was abolished when the blue livery was adopted, and

70

it was hard to get used to the disappearance of this characteristic British railway practice that was familiar for such a long time.

In 1971 when the local railway network was given its own specific title, all the Southport and Wirral electric rolling stock was lettered MERSEYRAIL and a small square poster depicting a train with a smiling face was applied, but the latter evidently proved unpopular and vanished overnight after a few months! Perhaps there was little to smile about with fares being ever on the increase!

A further livery change was begun in March, 1977, when a three-car set train was painted in the blue and grey "main line" style, and bore in addition to the British Rail logo, that of the Merseyside Passenger Transport Authority. It was however, some months before any further trains were so treated and eventually the blue and grey became the standard for the whole fleet.

A scene at Ormskirk station when it was still a busy terminus for electric trains and an interchange station for trains to Rainford Junction and Southport. A train of 1927 stock stands at the main-line platform, Summer, 1955.

(Photo: R. Stephens)

Ormskirk station looking North in pre-World War 1 days. A steam rail-motor unit stands in the bay, used on the Aintree service before the line was electrified.
(Photo: J. Ryan collection)

Ormskirk station looking North, July, 1984. A Class 508 train (508.110) on loan from the Wirral lines meets up with a diesel unit on the Preston service. The Liverpool and Preston lines are separated by buffers, but an emergency loop links both lines. (Photo: S.G. Jones)

Exploring the Lines — By Train

Recalling typical train journeys on both the Southport and Ormskirk lines would appear to be the best way of describing them, but descriptions dated for the present time would give no hint of what the lines were like in their heyday. Drastic alterations have been made in post-war years, more particularly since the mid-1960's so any description, to be of any use, must be back-dated 20 years or so. Probably the best way of accomplishing the task is to make a couple of imaginary train journeys — say in the year 1962 before too much had gone, noting the sights and sounds that were there to be savoured by the interested observer, then bring the picture up to date by subsequent references.

In a similar manner to that of our hypothetical passenger of the 1850's, we find ourselves walking along Moorfields, Liverpool, with ahead of us a very different Exchange station to that which our predecessor entered to commence his journey to Southport. Facing us is the long-familiar, blackened facade of the station and hotel, built in the mid-1880's to replace the original, smaller station which became inadequate for the expanding traffic. The present station has ten very long platforms, numbers 7 to 10 being used exclusively by electric trains. An ornamental three-faced clock adorns the station portal — usually kept five minutes fast!

We cross Tithebarn Street and pass through the main entrance, reaching the concourse via the taxi rank, next bearing left in order to reach the appropriate ticket office. At this time the local lines have a separate office, main-line tickets being issued at an adjacent one. The time of the next train to Southport and its platform number is ascertained by reference to the large illuminated train indicator with its row of clock faces which is suspended from the station roof girders.

The entrance through which we have just passed was made when the old station was demolished and its replacement made twice as wide, extending to Pall Mall. This work involved the demolition of many houses and the obliteration of two streets. The main station entrance covers what was formerly the spot at which Key Street met Tithebarn Street.

The train for Southport is standing at Platform 9, its sliding doors open to receive passengers, filling up gradually as people stream through the ticket barrier, and, making their way to their favourite positions in the coaches, settle down for the journey. Later comers are apt to miss their favourite seats. In the intervening time until departure we can observe the various train movements within the station — electric trains arriving, steam trains to and from Preston or North-East Lancashire arriving or departing, and diesel train sets on the Bolton and Manchester services. This is a transitional time, when there are still quite a large number of steam locomotives at work, and up at the top end of the station the "pilot" engine simmers quietly, awaiting its next task. Perhaps this will be the removal of empty carriages from a train lately arrived, or detachment from such a train of vans to be shunted into the bay or to another platform. Today the engine is one of the small 2-6-2 Tank design of the 412XX series which were introduced by the LMS company in 1947. This is the class most frequently employed nowadays on Exchange station duties, but occasionaly one of the larger Stanier 2-6-4 Tank engines, or a BR Standard Class 4 4-6-0 may be used. In days only recently past the work was carried out by the long familiar Aspinall 2-4-2 Tank engines, or if on a rare occasion one of these numerous and trusty machines was not available one of the 0-6-0 goods engines would be pressed into service. These latter locomotives always looked rather out of place in a terminal station. After 1947 the LMS Standard Class 2P 4-4-0's put in a period of station pilot work here, at a time when pre-Grouping engines were becoming scarcer month by month due to withdrawals of older machines, many of which had been given an extended lease of life due to the war. On watching the pilot engine at work one reflects on the fact that soon all steam locomotives will be gone. In spite of early electrification, Liverpool Exchange station still sees more steam locomotives than either Lime Street or Central — both the latter having been steam strongholds until recently. Exchange has a distinct atmosphere of its own — the pre-Group era seems to linger on despite many changes. The station even has its own particular aroma, a delicious one (to the true railway lover) of steam and coal smoke, nowadays having become mixed with diesel fumes and the effluvia of various neighbouring industries as might be expected with the station being situated on the edge of a large industrial district.

To revert to the journey — although it is as yet only mid-afternoon, a goodly number of passengers make for the Southport train, but the real rush begins about 4.30 p.m. when the business day is drawing to a close; between that hour and about 6.30 p.m. the throng is enormously increased and the trains are packed to capacity. They are fairly busy all day however, even though bus competition and that from private cars exists in plenty. The latter is, however, having an effect on the buses as well as the trains, but traffic congestion is a drawback to motoring and, coupled with car parking problems, many motorists find the train a good mode of travel to and from Liverpool or Southport. The trains provide speedy journeys which the buses, and often cars, cannot match. On sunny Sundays and Bank holidays in the Summer, traffic has at times built up to such a pitch that extra booking facilities have had to be provided. Small huts on wheels are trundled out into the station concourse at such times, in which perspiring clerks have sold thousands of tickets for Southport and other popular places along the line. At times of exceptionally heavy traffic, short workings of trains have been introduced to clear homecoming passengers from intermediate stations who would have no chance of boarding already full trains returning from Southport. Increasing car ownership is however, decreasing this holiday-time traffic.

Shouts of "any more for Southport" from the gatemen and the crash of platform barriers being slammed shut herald the moment of departure and, in response to the pressing of a button switch by the guard, the doors on every car of the train rumble shut simultaneously, but occasionally a door sticks and a second try has to be made. The introduction of sliding doors brought occasional problems — obstructions in the form of litter, particularly such things as cherry stones when untidy passengers throw these on the floor and they get stuck in the door channels. Sometimes too, a hurrying girl passenger will leave a styletto-heeled shoe behind as she steps into or out of the train — that door channel again! Nevertheless the sliding doors certainly speeded up loading and unloading at the intermediate stations, and prevented impatient passengers from leaping off the train before it has come to a halt, as used to happen on the former L & Y trains with their manual doors.

After closing the doors the guard signals "two bells" to the driver, on receipt of which, and provided that the starting signal is showing clear, he notches round the controller handle and the train commences yet another of its countless journeys. As the train picks up speed the wheel flanges whine with a low note on the sharp curvature of the rails and hammer their way through the numerous points and crossing frogs that make up the complex of trackwork at the station approach. On leaving Liverpool Exchange we note the two large signal boxes that control the traffic into and out of the busy terminal with its complicated "floor" as signalmen describe the track under their jurisdiction. On our right just beyond the platform end is Liverpool Exchange No. 2 — a long, characteristically L & Y design timber box on a brickwork base, which dates from earlier days. On the left-hand side just beyond the former junction with the high-level goods lines is a new, modernistic flat-roofed timber signal box — Liverpool Exchange No. 1, which has been built to replace an elevated box of L & Y origin mounted on steel gantries and which, until recently stood on the East side of the track here, and in its latter years had a pronounced sag in the middle! The colour-light signalling at Liverpool Exchange station dates from 1937 and replaced the multiplicity of old L & Y semaphores which, on their various combinations of posts and brackets gave a great deal of character to the scene here.

Southport line trains negotiate a sharp reverse curve upon leaving Exchange station, with a gentler curve as far out as Sherwood Street, a distance of about three-quarters of a mile. This stretch is awkward

75

to negotiate and speed is kept low between Exchange and a point beyond Liverpool Exchange Junction, where the track straightens out. The curvaceous course followed by the line was dictated by the fact that the railway had to thread its way through an already built-up area nearer the town, whereas there was little in the way of streets and buildings beyond the town limits when the line was constructed, so that a more direct route was possible once the already established streets and buildings had been left behind.

The train proceeds along the four-tracked viaduct taking the extreme left-hand line in the shadow of tall mills and warehouses, speed being slow due to the permanent restriction that applies to this section of track. The controller handle is in the series position, the traction motors hum a low tune and the collector shoes strike sparks from the live rail. After passing Liverpool Exchange Junction signal box, an LMS design timber building on the Down side which replaced a former L & Y box that was destroyed in the wartime "blitz", and at which the Great Howard Street goods lines join the main tracks, the railway makes its last curve and straightens out. The signal box just referred to is now mis-named, for the junction and the goods lines are now out of use. Below the viaduct on the Down side, the desolate remains of Great Howard Street goods station bear witness to the traffic decline, cars and lorries now being parked on land which was until recently the preserve of railway wagons. The "enemy" is certainly well entrenched here! Far below in a deep cutting the ex-L & NWR Waterloo Dock Branch can be glimpsed briefly as it passes beneath Great Howard Street yard. There were formerly three levels of railway at this interesting point, namely the main lines up on the viaduct, goods lines in the yards below, and lower still, the ex-L & NWR Waterloo Dock line.

The odours of a variety of industries intrude as we pass by factories and mills, but they are soon forgotten in the contemplation of the passing scene. To our left Bibby's enormous seed and soap mills, Stanley Dock tobacco warehouse, Clarence Dock power station, narrow streets, tall warehouses of various vintages; to the right the extensive steam shrouded sugar refineries and the multitude of streets rising towards Everton. The skyline in that direction is now altering as old, squalid housing gives way to flats and tower blocks, with St. George's church at the highest point providing a contrast from the old world. Further onwards the canal locks are crossed by the railway and the gasholders of Atholl Street come into view on the right. The district is a fantastic mixture of industrial buildings, warehouses, tenements new and not so new, ancient four-roomed houses in narrow streets and a panorama of cranes and ships in the docks to the West of the line. St. Alban's church with its square tower, looking like a village church, nestles among the industry on the Down side of the railway where it crosses Denbigh Street and Bentinck Street. Most of this district received a severe pounding from bombing during the air-raiding period of 1940-41 and many of the new buildings to be seen have replaced structures which were reduced to heaps of broken bricks and twisted steel. The areas of new brickwork on many of the warehouses where demolished sections have been rebuilt are a constant reminder of the wartime period when the railways of Liverpool and Bootle were literally in the front line of battle, especially the tracks between Liverpool Exchange and Seaforth which, being so close to the North Docks, received a severe hammering from enemy bombers crewed by men whose mission was to destroy the docks and their transportation lifelines. The railway viaduct was badly damaged, parts being completely destroyed and many months of work were required to rebuild it. Temporary timber trestle bridges were constructed to carry the Southport line, over which Ormskirk trains were also operated, all main-line trains being terminated at Kirkdale, passengers transferring to special buses or Ormskirk line trains for journeys to and from Liverpool Exchange. From 18th August, 1941 some steam trains were run through to Exchange but normal operation was not resumed until late in 1942.

During the period of air raiding the Southport line services were kept going somehow, but inevitably some interuptions occured, and on one or two occasions when the power supply was affected, steam trains were run in place of electric trains. Of course, when the viaduct was out of use Southport line trains were forced to terminate at Sandhills for a time, with bus connections for Liverpool. Damage to track and bridges in Liverpool and Bootle was so severe that in addition to the buses a special train service was operated between Liverpool Central station and Southport Lord Street by the Cheshire Lines Committee from 24th December, 1940 until 5th July, 1941 in order to assist the LMS company. This was in addition to the ordinary but somewhat sparse service on the CLC line. Nevertheless, in spite of one setback after another coupled with destruction of equipment on a large scale, the services were kept going in one form or another by quick thinking, hard work, smart planning and improvisation. Apart from the severe disruption caused by demolished bridgework it was seldom that service interuptions were more than of a few hours duration, for bomb craters were quickly filled-in, rails relaid and trains passing over once again, but at reduced speed until the ground had consolidated. It was all in the days (or nights) work during that stormy era!

Having digressed in recalling the past, our train has meanwhile reached the straight section of track beyond the speed restriction and the driver notches the controller handle round to the full-parallel position causing the train to surge forward with terrific acceleration, the motor hum rising to a high pitched whine, but the exhilarating burst of high speed is short lived and the brakes go on hard for the stop at Sandhills station. The automatic doors rumble open and more passengers come aboard, whilst one or two alight.

Huskisson goods station and railway yards are spread before us on the right-hand side at a much lower level. This depot was built by the Cheshire Lines Committee and is at the end of a branch line from Walton-on-the-Hill which reaches Sandhills via cuttings and tunnels, emerging near Kirkdale station, which is on the Ormskirk line, and runs parallel with the latter but deep down. It is interesting to see engines from the former London & North Eastern Railway in Huskisson yard, many miles from their own system.

Sandhills station is not the original one, but dates from the widening of the lines to four tracks in the 1880's. The present station has three platforms, one of them being a rather narrow island. The Down platform is of brick construction, but the island and Up platforms are timber-built, and so are all the platform buildings, and by the early 1960's the whole station had reached a grim state of dinginess and dilapidation. The Down platform received a new timber awning (which was supported by a centre timber "wall" with alcoves). The station now has electric lighting but on the whole is a depressing structure which is not improved by continual vandalism and defacement, quite apart from the effects of industrial polution and the weather.

Passing behind the Down platform at Sandhills is the four-tracked North Docks Branch, which was opened in 1855 to serve coal tips at Wellington and Bramley-Moore Docks, and the goods station at Blackstone Street, the latter which is at roadway level and reached via a steep incline. Looking Westwards here a vista of cranes, warehouses and ships funnels meets the eyes, whilst Eastwards are the tracks leading into Huskisson goods station, with industrial buildings of great variety in the background.

On those occasions when a steam train and an electric train are scheduled to leave Exchange station at the same time, the latter usually gets ahead due to the smart acceleration characteristics of electric traction, but the steam train will not be far behind. When the electric train has drawn up at Sandhills station the passengers are treated to the spectacle of the steam train passing through at speed (unless that too is scheduled to stop there), a sight that compels many of the avid newspaper readers to raise their eyes for a moment! In pre-war days many of the Southport and Ormskirk trains had simultaneous departure times from Liverpool Exchange station, but after the introduction of the compartment type trains it was the older L & Y sets that lost the race to Sandhills. Today there are diesel train sets to add spice to the competition and sometimes one of these manages to keep ahead of an electric train should the latter leave the station a few seconds late. When it comes to acceleration and swift getaway from stops, the electric trains are vastly superior, however.

On leaving Sandhills extensive coal sidings overlooked by the enormous warehouses of Juniper, Miskelly and Barr Streets, and numerous old industrial buildings are seen on the Down side, also the Leeds & Liverpool Canal which passes beneath the railway here. Further sidings and a single-line branch to the North Shore Mill (which diverges in a trailing direction on the Up side) are a part of the scene on looking to the right. There are eight parallel sets of rails here, in addition to numerous sidings. Prior to 1937 two fairly large signal boxes, Sandhills No's 1 and 2 stood on the Up side only a few-hundred yards apart. These were replaced by the present Sandhills No. 1 signal box under the re-signalling scheme of that year. This newer box stands on the Up side of the line immediately on the Liverpool side of the canal bridge, which is almost a tunnel, as all eight tracks cross the waterway on a series of plate-girder bridges side-by-side.

The aforementioned coal sidings curve away to the left on the Down side, the most distant siding being on the bank of the canal, on which there are several coal tipping appliances (now disused) by which coal was unloaded from railway wagons into barges for transport to various industrial premises and gas works that do not possess rail connections. Shunting in these extensive sidings is performed by steam locomotives. The Southport line diverges from the main Northbound lines at Bank Hall and curves away sharply to the left, which route our train now takes, its wheel flanges grinding on the rails as it turns. The many sidings on our left end in stop-blocks near the wall below Bank Hall Street, a busy road which passes over the line by a recently reconstructed bridge. Immediately beyond this bridge are the platforms of Bank Hall station, which is the most gloomy one on the whole line! Massively constructed, this station is built of timber, sandstone, and those characteristic L & Y Railway yellow bricks, with plenty of ornamental ironwork in the best Victorian railway tradition. There are two long island platforms, and a high brick retaining wall adjacent to the Up line. On the Down side is open land, with several sidings for stabling electric trains in off-peak periods. A short distance beyond Bank Hall station is the site of the long-vanished station of Miller's Bridge, which was opened in 1850 and closed in 1876. The track between Bank Hall and Seaforth was quadrupled during the years 1886-7.

The district of Bank Hall was named after an ancient manor house which once stood amid delightful surroundings of fields and hedgerows, with the River Mersey nearby and a vista of the Wirral shore beyond. The hall was demolished about the year 1772, but traces of it remained until a century later when industrialisation of the district had begun. The traveller standing on Bank Hall station in the 1960's would find it difficult to visualise the scenes of old, as there is not even a·tree in sight! The whole area surrounding the station was built over, more than a century ago, in the usual town manner, with narrow streets of small terraced houses and a multitude of industrial premises. Nowadays however, new and rebuilt structures are altering the scenes of yesteryear. The station was opened in 1870 to serve the developing district, and has grown old and gloomy along with its surroundings. Indeed, the posters displayed on the station hoardings impart the only touches or colour and brightness to the scene!

Between Bank Hall and Bootle (Oriel Road) stations, the railway runs at a level that is only a little above the street, but gradually rises through Bootle on embankments. Four running lines continue as far as Seaforth, with a loop on the Down side near Bank Hall. The ex-L &NWR Edge Hill-Alexandra Dock Branch emerges from a tunnel, climbing a steep gradient to run parallel with the L & Y line on the Up side, at the same level. A crossover connection between the two railways was installed here in 1886, known as Bootle Junction, and both companies provided their own signal box to control it, but in LMS days the L & NWR box was abolished and all the points and signals placed under the control of the L & Y box which still exists and is one of that company's standard all-timber structures, situated on the Down side of the Southport line. Beyond Bootle Junction the L & NW line descends steeply into a cutting and turns Westwards to pass beneath the L & Y lines near Bootle (Oriel Road) station. In the L & NW cutting we see the forlorn remains of Bootle (Balliol Road) station, closed for many years. Passengers bound for Southport from the Bootle Branch trains changed at Balliol Road and reached the L & Y Oriel Road station via a long sloping footpath and a short walk along the public road. For years after the Bootle Branch local passenger trains ceased to operate (in May, 1948) a weathered sign stood on Balliol Road station reading TO THE ELECTRIC TRAINS. Almost opposite the two stations stands the grey, dignified Bootle Town Hall with its handsome clock tower, which was completed in 1886, a year in which the L & Y Company carried out several important improvement schemes on Merseyside.

Oriel Road station is a very large one, situated slightly above street level with a covered cab rank, also a bus turning circle in the forecourt, used by buses on Liverpool Corporation's Route No. 60 — Bootle to Aigburth, one of the oldest bus routes in the city, which commenced with open-top solid-tyred vehicles in the early 1920's. Every generation of Liverpool bus has stood outside Oriel Road station over the years. Now looking every bit its age, the railway station was opened as far back as 1876, replacing the former stations of Miller's Bridge and Bootle Village. The latter was situated a little distance further North near the present Merton Road bridge. Just like Bank Hall, Oriel Road station is built largely of yellow glazed bricks so characteristic of the old L & Y, and with an over-abundance of roofing supported on numerous iron columns. A subway connects the platforms, of which there are four, one being a wide island. The extreme Down side platform, now disused, was formerly served by the local electric trains which ran between Liverpool Exchange and Aintree via Marsh Lane Junction until 1951. The ex-L & Y signal box which stands on the Down side of the railway at the North end of the platform is named simply Bootle Station. Four tracks pass through the station, whilst the double track goods line to Bankfield passes behind a wall on the station's West side and descends into a cutting to make its way to the docks. It leaves the Southport line at the North end of Oriel Road station. We have to note all the forgoing items quickly, as the trains travel at a rapid pace between Bank Hall and Bootle stations, the wheels making a fine clatter on the trackwork of Bootle Junction as they encounter several points and crossings.

On leaving Bootle station the railway crosses the wide Merton Road by a plate-girder bridge, next crossing the Leeds & Liverpool Canal yet again. Electric power lines on tall lattice gantries straddle the canal here and are a familiar feature of the Bootle landscape. Streets of older houses and industrial premises are mixed willy-nilly in the district through which the railway is now passing on a fairly high embankment, the line having been raised from ground level during the 1880's in order to eliminate level crossings. Soon the train comes to a halt at Marsh Lane & Strand Road station, on the South side of Marsh Lane, which, opened on 11th April 1886 replaced an earlier station which was on the North side of that thoroughfare. Once similar in design and amenities to Bootle (Oriel Road), it is now greatly altered due to results of the wartime blitz, when it was completely destroyed in May, 1941. After this event, the station was out of use until July 1943 when it was re-opened, devoid of any platform buildings. In 1945 pre-fabricated waiting shelters were added so that the station has a decidedly modern look in great contrast to its neighbours that escaped serious damage. Up on the embankment and reached by long sloping covered footways, the station overlooks a mixed industrial and residential area, with the enormous Linacre Road gas works nearby. Far below, the ex-Midland Railway goods branch from Fazakerley North Junction to Langton Dock emerges from its tunnel into a deep cutting below street level and passes beneath Marsh Lane station. Here some quite spectacular stone and brick archwork carries the L & Y lines high above the Langton Dock Branch. On the Down side beyond Marsh Lane bridge (plate-girder) a coal depot and goods yard with a number of sidings is situated at street level, the approach track descending to reach it via a long incline.

The four tracks continue beyond Marsh Lane station, still on the embankment and passing through a mixed residential and industrial district of mainly nineteenth-century development. A short distance onwards two sets of rails branch from the main lines on the Down side near Marsh Lane Junction signal box, an ex-L & Y structure which is also on the Down side on the South side of the plater-girder bridge that crosses Knowsley Road, Bootle. The branching tracks climb to a still higher level and, turning Eastwards, cross the Southport line and adjacent land on a viaduct with plate-girder spans and brick arches, and joins the Aintree-North Mersey line which also crosses above the Southport line via a plate-girder bridge, both lines merging at North Mersey Branch Junction which lies to the East of the Southport line. The junction signal box can be seen on its high vantage point away to the right. The connection between the two lines was made in 1886, and was one of several new projects carried our in the 1880's to improve the handling of goods traffic in Liverpool and Bootle.

The inclined tracks are used mainly by transfer goods trains between Aintree and Edge Hill, and by certain express goods trains between the latter place and Carlisle, or Carnforth, in the Northbound direction only — there are no regular corresponding Southbound workings. The use of this route for Edge Hill-Carlisle trains was instituted during the late war. There have been no regular passenger trains over the North Mersey line between Marsh Lane Junction and Aintree since the electric trains between Liverpool Exchange and the latter place (via Marsh Lane) were withdrawn in 1951. Special "Grand National" passenger trains from London and the Midlands have been routed this way in recent years, which traverse the Southport line between Bootle Junction and Marsh Lane Junction on the day of the famous race, which in post-war years has been held on a Saturday.

Having passed beneath the aforementioned bridges in quick succession, the train next arrives at Seaforth & Litherland station. There have been considerable changes effected to the railway layout in this area since 1963 and it is necessary to look at the situation as it was prior to that year in order to appreciate the importance that Seaforth station once had in the local transport scene. Seaforth South signal box, a large one of L & Y vintage was situated in the middle of the four tracks and controlled the junction with the double track line that was used by the Liverpool Overhead Railway, which entered the station via a sweeping West-North curve. The LOR system was closed on 30th December, 1956, but the rails were left in position, unused, for quite a long time afterwards, becoming black with rust and hidden by grass and weeds. Seaforth & Litherland station itself, built on the embankment was large and commodious, constructed entirely of timber and possessing four platforms (two side and an island), and was well provided with waiting rooms etc., also awnings to shelter waiting passengers. The no-longer existing Down-side platform was burnt away during an air raid, but it had seen little use for some years beforehand. The station platforms are reached via lengthy sloping covered footways which give access from Seaforth Road.

The closure of the Liverpool Overhead Railway and reduction of train services through Seaforth reduced line occupation to such an extent that the four tracks were considered to be no longer necessary and they have been reduced to two only beyond Marsh Lane

Junction. This work, carried out during 1963 involved removal of the outer lines leaving the former inner tracks to becomes Up and Down main lines. The area was also re-signalled and Seaforth South signal box abolished. Removal of the line to Seaforth Sands, formerly used by the "Overhead" trains was also carried out at this time, and the Up side platform at Seaforth & Litherland station was demolished leaving the island platform to serve trains in both directions.

Immediately beyond the station the railway crosses above Seaforth Road on two plate-girder bridges placed alongside each other, but each bridge now carries only a single line in place of two as was formerly the case. At street level, on the Down side a fairly large goods yard and coal depot existed until 1962, in which year it was closed, the rails being removed in the following year. Access to the yard was via a long approach siding that descended gradually to street level. At Seaforth North signal box, of the same design as its South neighbour stands at the Junction at which the four sets of rails formerly merged into two, and then the embankment gives way to a short stretch of railway more or less level with the houses on either side, followed by an earthen cutting. The new-looking bridge which spans the cutting was built in 1963 and replaced a former old stone hump-back bridge that connected Brook Vale and Sandy Road. A short run onwards brings the train to the sharply curved approach to Waterloo station, and here the Up and Down lines are placed fairly wide apart. Flange lubricators minimise the wear and the amount of screeching from the wheels as the train slows in order to observe the speed restriction which is permanently in force here. Ahead now is Crosby Road bridge which carries the highway over the line. The original bridge of 1850 is still in use, contiguous with the newer span which was added when track alterations were made and the present station built in 1879-81. The old bridge has rusticated sandstone abutments. Immediately beyond the bridge is Waterloo station at the South end of which, until electrification of the line there existed a small signal box known as Waterloo "B". It was situated at the platform end between the widely separated lines.

Waterloo station consists of a wide island platform, situated in a shallow earthen cutting, and serves a residential area that was developed over the second half of the last century. An open footbridge spans the railway at the Liverpool end of the station, and has a stairway connection with the platform. Ample waiting accommodation is provided on the platform, also a bookstall as befits the busiest station on the line, whilst at street level on South Road overbridge there is a booking office and a wide stairway for the entry and exit of passengers. There is also a luggage lift, as the platform is below street level.

The original station at Waterloo was on a different site, being situated alongside Brighton Road on land now occupied by the goods and coal yard. The railway passed over South Road via a level crossing before the present bridge was built, in 1881. Little development took place at Waterloo until some years after the railway was opened, and at first it was a quiet resort for the wealthy. This character changed in due course and building on a large scale developed. The nearby seashore provided an attraction for visitors, as it was a splendid place from which to observe shipping in the Crosby Channel, with the skyline of Liverpool to the South, the open sea to the North, whilst opposite lay the expanding resort of New Brighton with its fort and lighthouse to complete a pleasant vista.

As Waterloo station is an island, the Up and Down lines are still wide apart as they emerge from beneath South Road bridge with its two separate openings, and for many years there was a lengthy siding between the two tracks, with access from both, so that a train could be reversed here if necessary. It was removed during LMS days however. On the West side of the line lies the broad expanse of the goods and coal depot with its several sidings, paralleled by Brighton Road. This is not the original road of this name however, as the first Brighton Road was some distance North of Waterloo station and ran from West to East, from the sea front to Crosby Road, the railway crossing it on the level, of which more later. At the present time the goods depot deals mainly with domestic coal traffic, little general merchandise being dealt with nowadays. The yard is of considerable length and contains five sidings, and a long headshunt.

At the extreme end of Waterloo goods yard is St. John's Road level crossing with its adjacent ex-L & Y signal box which is on the Down side immediately on the station side of the crossing, and is named simply Waterloo. Three sets of rails pass over the roadway, the two main tracks and the head-shunt of the goods sidings. A point of interest concerning St. John's Road crossing lies in the gates being operated by an electric motor, which was installed as long ago as 1906 in place of the more usual large diameter hand-wheel turned by the signalman.

It is a fairly long stretch between Waterloo and the next station, Blundellsands & Crosby, and trains travel at a fast speed over this section of line, which is at the same level as the surrounding land, the cuttings and embankments having now been left behind us. The residential nature of the district is well apparent, with houses large and small, of old and modern designs flanking the railway on either side. Another level crossing is passed over at Brook Road East, but the signal box, which is an ex-L & Y one closely adjacent to 1920's houses and situated on the Down side at the north end of the crossing bears the title Brook Hall Road. This crossing apparently replaced an earlier one situated at Brighton Road, which was done away with. We noted earlier that the present Brighton Road is at Waterloo, the original one having been renamed Jubilee Road, a title which it still bears, and comes to an abrupt end at the railway wall, having been

84

blanked off when the newer crossing at Brook Road was installed. The older crossing was a little distance further North than the present one.

Our train is still travelling fast making detailed observation difficult, but soon the brakes go on at the approaches to Blundellsands & Crosby station, and after passing under Mersey Road bridge, the station platforms are reached and the train halts. Many passengers alight here and more board the train, as the station is an extremely busy one. It has the usual Up and Down platforms, the Down side buildings being of brick and stone construction and both having substantial awnings. The Up side buildings are of timber construction by way of contrast. Alterations have been carried out here over the years resulting in enlargement of the passenger accommodation. Until recent times ample provision for goods and mineral traffic was a feature of Crosby station. Behind the Down platform there was a goods and coal yard with sidings and a large rectangular water tank. The headshunt of this yard, a single long siding extended for a considerable distance alongside the walls of the fine large houses in Merilocks Road, with their tree-shaded gardens. In 1953 this siding was shortened, and this was the beginning of the end, for ten years later the yard was closed and all the rails removed.

On the Up side of the line several sidings were provided, but these too were removed in the early 1960's, and the large signal box (ex-L & Y) has had many of its levers rendered spare through the abolition of points and signals relating to the former sidings. Today the signal box looks rather lonely since the several lines that passed in front of it have been cleared away.

The area of Crosby in which the station is situated consisted of only a few cottages at the time the railway was built, but development was fairly rapid after the line was opened and the village came within easy reach of Liverpool. The original station of 1848 was adjacent to what is now Mersey Road, but there was no overbridge, the railway passing over the road by a level crossing. The original station master's house still stands in Mersey Road but has long since passed out of railway use. The present station was built in 1852 and for many years there was a level crossing at the Liverpool end of the platforms, but this was replaced by the present subway for pedestrians only, at a later stage of development, and road traffic diverted onto Mersey Road via the bridge.

A run of about a mile amid a tree-shaded area of large houses of 1880's vintage brings our train to another station in Crosby which is entitled Hall Road, situated immediately beyond the level crossing which carries the last-named thoroughfare over the railway. A fairly large ex-L & Y signal box of Saxby & Farmer (signalling contractors) design stands on the Down side of the line at the South side of the road crossing and controls the gates, also numerous points and signals, for Hall Road is a very busy little railway centre situated on the fringe of urban development.

Hall Road passenger station was opened in 1874, after the district had begun to develop as a residential area. It has the usual Up and Down platforms, with small, neat red-brick waiting rooms and an open footbridge adjacent to the level crossing. Sand drifting along the road and railway proclaims its nearness to the seashore. The residential character of the land which has been such a feature all the way from Bootle changes abruptly here, for although the large houses stretch right up to the station on the Crosby side, beyond it are wide open spaces — to the left bracken-covered sand dunes and golf courses, whilst to the East more golf courses and fields with distant modern housing fill the view. Immediately adjacent to the station on its West side stands the large train servicing depot and workshop which was built in 1939-40, though stabling sidings and one or two smaller maintenance buildings existed on the site beforehand.

In previous years many trains were run between Liverpool and Hall Road only, and a special track arrangement enabled them to turn back without obstructing the running lines. Beyond the passenger station the Up and Down main lines are placed widely apart and a lengthy "middle road" is provided in between them. This is reached via facing points from the Down line, and enables a terminating train to be run directly into the siding to await its turn to go back to Liverpool, when it leaves via points connected to the Up line. Very few trains terminate at Hall Road nowadays however, so the siding is mainly used for holding trains between duties. Other sidings here are also used for stabling purposes, and it seems quite odd to see electric trains of a busy suburban railway standing amid sand dunes and open fields. A further installation at Hall Road is the electrical control room which is on the Up side of the line immediately beyond the station platforms. This was constructed after the 1939 war and does not date from the early electric days.

It is about one and three-quarter miles from Hall Road to the next station and trains travel along this stretch at high speed through open, almost flat land — fields and golf courses on the right, whilst sandhills covered with gorse and starr grass accompany the railway on the seaward side, the Mersey estuary, though close-by, not being visible on account of the dunes. The spire of Little Crosby church, and Ince Woods can be seen far across the fields, but suburbia is spreading and new houses are being built on some of the fields. We are now approaching Hightown, which belies its title for it is almost at sea level, and it the scene of plenty of residential development.

Hightown station is pleasantly situated on the North side of Alt Road level crossing, adjacent to which is the signal box, on the Up side, similar to design to that at Hall Road. Each platform has neat brick and stonework buildings. Goods facilities consist of a siding on the Down side and a small goods and coal yard on the Up side of the line, Southward of the level crossing. The latter rejoices in the title of Sniggery Siding, and was so named after the nearby Sniggery farm. Nearby, on the seaward side of the railway are the windswept, sandy reaches of Altcar rifle range, which will be vividly remembered by countless servicemen of two wars who had to endure the heat of Summer or the icy chill of Winter when undergoing their firing course. Large numbers of such personnel travelled to and from Hightown by train on these occasions. The range had its own station for many years, which was named Altcar Rifle Range Halt, but this fell in to disuse before World War 2, together with several sidings on the Down side of the line which gradually disappeared beneath drifting sand, but were occasionally dug out to accommodate Engineer's Department rolling stock. These sidings were originally provided for the Southport Sand Company. They were removed circa 1947. An extensive narrow-gauge railway system covered the firing range, the rolling stock consisting of hand-propelled trolleys. This also fell into disuse between the wars, but remnants of it remained for many years.

Continuing beyond Hightown the scenery still consists of sand - hills and fields, the latter flat and extensive stretching away Eastwards and resembling a Dutch landscape minus the windmills. A feature of the line for the next few miles is the number of unmanned level crossings serving minor roads and farm tracks, at which many a motor vehicle has met a destructive end over the years. The train next crosses the tidal estuary of the River Alt — little more than a wide stream — by a steel girder bridge, and prominent here in the flat landscape, on the East side stands the forlorn building of Formby power station, now used as a factory. Once it hummed with power as the generators produced the volts for the electrified lines, but as already recorded, was shut down in 1946. In the days when the power station was in use, a small platform was provided for the convenience of members of the staff travelling to or from work by train. The area surrounding the building is now quite desolate and weed-grown, with odd lengths of disconnected track meandering through the grass and undergrowth, a far cry from the days when the power station was the nerve centre of both the Southport and Ormskirk electrified lines.

Having passed the erstwhile power station, the train next passes rows of new or recently built houses, and shortly reaches Raven Meols Lane level crossing, with its ex-L & Y signal box which is on the Down side and bears the title of Eccles Crossing. In earlier days a smaller signal box controlled the crossing. It too, was on the Down side, but on the opposite side of the roadway (the present box is on the North side of Raven Meols Lane). A small goods yard with a single siding was, until recently, situated on the Down side beyond the level crossing but this was closed and the rails, with the exception of the points at the lead-in, removed during 1959. The goods crane stood forlornly for some time after the rails had gone, overlooking hordes of motor vehicles that were parked in the yard in consequence of it having become a car park.

Although the surrounding area is at the same level as the railway in this district, the train passes beneath an overbridge as it enters Formby station, 11½ miles from Liverpool. This is a fairly small station with Up and Down side platforms with waiting rooms on each, the main ticket office being up on the road bridge. Nearby is the inevitable Railway Hotel and its sign is of considerable interest to railway enthusiasts, as it bears a splendid painting of an early 0-6-0 type locomotive. Harking back to the station, we note how pleasant it is, being embellished with flower beds and ornamental effects by the staff in marked contrast to its predecessor of 1848 which lasted, with modifications, until 1913, the present station being built during that year. The original station was cramped and inconvenient, there being a station house, and a waiting room with an ungainly wooden awning on the Up platform, and only a small timber waiting shed on the opposite side. An open-air footbridge connected the platforms whilst the main road passed over the railway via a level crossing. The signal box was on the Up side, situated between the platform ramp and the roadway. The present bridge replaced the level crossing, the road being raised to pass above the railway.

Behind the platform and the trees on the Up side of the station there are several sidings for goods and coal traffic, in a picturesque location. The signal box, an ex-L & Y structure just North of the Down platform, is opened when the sidings are being shunted. The sidings lead from a very lengthy loop line known as Barkfield Siding, that stretches for three-quarters of a mile to the next station, which is Freshfield, the track being overshadowed by trees for most of the distance. At the latter place it branches into further sidings that are used for loading sand, formerly for the Southport Sand Company, but now for British Railways. Steel hopper wagons can usually be seen here with the instruction "Return to Freshfield" lettered on their sides, but a couple of strays from other BR sand pits may turn up occasionally, from Leighton Buzzard for instance!

Freshfield station is a rather small one, and was opened in 1854. It has two platforms and buildings of timber, and is situated pleasantly amid a wooded, sandy area. It is believed that when the station was built there was no name for it, there being then no village by the line, so some genius suggested it be called Freshfield because an adjacent field was owned by a Mr. Fresh! There is a level crossing at the South end of the station with its attendant ex-L & Y signal box on the Down side. Also, on that side behind the station is a small goods yard with several sidings. A long road, partly sand-covered and passing amid pine woods leads from the station to the shore, and in Summer many visitors alight from the trains, destined for a dusty walk to the beach.

Between Freshfield and Ainsdale, the sand hills are ever-present, with pine woods further North and fields stretching away to the East of the railway. Soon the train passes a small aerodome, which is on the East side of the line, and although the railway is signalled by the long familiar semaphores, unlit colour-light signals will be noted. These are provided to protect trains should an aircraft overshoot the field and obstruct the railway, in which event a stop aspect would be given by illumination of the signal through the errant aeroplane fouling trip wires. Beyond the airfield the abutments of the now vanished plate-girder bridge that carried the CLC. Aintree-Southport line over the L & Y track still remain in position — the section beyond Woodvale CLC station was closed in 1952. Immediately past the bridge is the site of the former Marshall's Siding, which was on the West side of the line.

Ainsdale, of the golden sands, is the next station we reach. It is a small one with brick platforms and timber buildings, serving a popular resort which for years has been a favourite place for day trippers to visit, whilst also being residential. At the North end of the station a level crossing takes the railway over Shore Road, controlled by an ex-L & Y signal box of Saxby & Farmer design.

Immediately North of the level crossing, on the East side, a single line curves sharply in a North-Easterly direction and leads to a small goods and coal yard. This siding is a remnant of a branch line that was built under an Act of 20th August, 1853, its purpose being to reach the Ainsdale Corn Mill which was situated about three-quarters of a mile away. The mill chimney can be seen from the train. This branch crossed Liverpool Road South on the level and, upon reaching the mill split into two long sidings leading to different parts of the establishment. The branch ceased to be used about the time of the second World War and the rails were eventually removed beyond the goods yard. Part of the course of the line has since been covered by new housing, whilst the mill is destined to be demolished.

The sandhills and woods continue as far as Hillside, where the built-up suburbs of Southport begin. Several level crossings are next encountered, and a large sub-station of classical "early electric" era design is prominent on the Up side of the line on the approach to Hillside station. A tiny hut with a nameboard attached lettered Lloyds & Siding, standing lonesomely on a nicely levelled stretch of cinders is mute evidence that goods traffic was once dealt with here. The little hut was a signal box of the ground-frame type, and is situated on the Up side.

Hillside passenger station, with concrete platforms, has its ticket office on a road overbridge. The station was a latecomer, not being built until 1926 when the district had become well developed for residential purposes. Like Sandhills, its name belies its location as there are no hills of any kind in the vicinity. From Hillside onwards

89

the railway, still at roadway level passes through a built-up area and presently crosses Crescent Road by a busy level crossing which is accompanied by an imported ex-Midland Railway signal box, which is named Eastbourne Road, situated on the Down side on the South side of the crossing. We are now in the district of Birkdale, one that became residential soon after the railway was opened, many of the "Merchant Princes" establishing homes in the vicinity. The present Birkdale station was opened in 1851, and replaced that of 1848 which was on a different site — it was actually situated between Sheringham Road and Dunkirk Road. The newer station was obviously designed to be a fitting amenity, being both substantial and ornate, with iron columns supporting platform awnings. Sidings for goods traffic are provided on the Up side at the South end of the station, whilst a level crossing exists at the North end with an adjacent ex-L & Y signal box of a design differing from any other on the Southport line. In order to give the signalman a clearer view of the station area, the box had its upper floor widened. It carries the title Liverpool Road. More sidings exist on the Down side of the line and extend as far as Aughton Road level crossing, at which there is a signal box with Midland Railway features, bearing the title of that thoroughfare. This crossing was formerly of rare distinction, for a single line electric tramway passed over the railway here, one of the few instances in Britain of a street tramway crossing a main-line railway on the same level, and possibly the only example in the country of one crossing an electrified railway? Both tramway and railway were fully protected by signals. The interest of this location diminished when the Southport tramways were closed in the year 1933.

Still travelling through a built-up residential district, our train passes over two further level crossings, first Duke Street, then Portland Street, each of which is controlled by a signal box of standard L & Y style, and each bearing the name of the crossing. After passing the site of the original terminal station at Eastbank Street, Southport South Junction is reached, with its larger version of the standard ex-L & Y signal box, which is on the Up side of the line. Here the line divides, the sharp curve to the left leading into Southport Chapel Street station, that to the right (the Southport Fork Line) providing an avoiding route which joins the main line running Eastwards from Southport, at St. Luke's. The train now traverses the left-hand curve, its wheel flanges whining dully, and runs into the terminal station after a journey that has lasted just about 40 minutes. Adjacent platforms accommodate steam trains, also DMU trains on local service between Southport and Wigan, Manchester etc., also certain long-distance trains at appropriate times of the day.

Southport Chapel Street is another example of a former L & Y - style sandstone and yellow-brick station, the platform area being similar in design to Liverpool Exchange, though smaller. It is situated in a busy shopping centre with no industrial smoke or harmful pollution to blacken it as has been the case at Liverpool over the years, but the old stone frontage block now looks its age with the effects of time, wind and weather. The station, which was opened in 1851, was enlarged and improved during 1901. There are 11 platforms under an overall roof of the "train shed" type, and two long, completely open excursion platforms at London Street out beyond the main station on the North side of the railway. The platforms are numbered 1 to 10 and although there are eleven actual platform faces, there is none now bearing the number 11. The former No. 11 was a short bay on the North side once used by the Downholland Branch trains, which were discontinued in 1938. The excursion platforms are numbered 12 and 13.

The London Street side of Chapel Street station was originally the terminus of the East Lancashire Railway Company's line from Manchester, and was opened in 1855. Chapel Street was the intended terminus of the Liverpool, Crosby & Southport Railway, the land upon which the station was built being conveniently vacant, but as already noted, a temporary station at Eastbank Street was used until the main station at Chapel Street was completed. It is well situated, quite near Southport's chief thoroughfare, the magnificent and stylish Lord Street.

The temporary Eastbank Street station was a little way out of the town, and little trace of it can be discerned today apart from the stationmaster's house, which still stands, and a small building adjacent to Portland Street level crossing, which was probably a booking office. Eastbank Street today is a busy thoroughfare, which climbs to cross the railway via an iron bridge.

Although Chapel Street station has always handled a vast amount of holiday traffic, the coming of the railway, whilst not being the cause of Southport becoming a resort (it was already one in pre-railway days) certainly set the town on the road to swift development and progress, and was the means of tremendously increasing the number of visitors. People came to Southport by canal barge and road coach in the days before the railways were built, but in comparatively small numbers. Southport received far more visitors than Blackpool until the 1870's, and had a greater population than its more Northerly rival which however, developed into a "holiday factory" leaving Southport as a more sedate resort, fittingly referred to as the "Garden City", and described as such in the advertising of the Cheshire Lines Railway which also served the resort, though no connection was ever made between the two railway systems within the town.

The railway traffic of Chapel Street station can be observed splendidly from the long Victoria footbridge, an open lattice structure which crosses all main tracks and sidings and links streets on either side of the railway, but does not provide access to the platforms, being situated well outside the station precincts although the London Street excursion platforms pass beneath it. The ironwork of the bridge was made by S & N Newell & Company of Darlington, in 1878. Since the abolition of steam locomotives and the reduction in train services there is little of interest to see nowadays from this vantage point.

The signalling in the vicinity of Chapel Street station is a mixture of standard upper-quadrant semaphores, old L & Y semaphores and recently installed colour-light signals. The semaphore signals and points are operated by an electro-pnuematic system that was installed as long ago as 1919, and the fierce hiss as a signal arm moves or points-blades is, along with the hum of traction motors, a characteristic Chapel Street station sound. The main signal box towers to a considerable height above the station approach tracks adjacent to the curve traversed by the Liverpool-Southport trains, and is not of the familiar L & Y standard design but is an oddity among the surrounding buildings which are in the typical L & Y style of architecture.

The Liverpool electric trains use platforms Nos. 1 to 3 at Chapel Street. A siding, complete with an inspection pit between the rails, is situated alongside No. 1 platform line and enables examinations to be made and routine tasks to be carried out such as the changing of brake blocks, without the necessity for a train going to Hall Road or Meols Cop works for such attention. This siding accommodated steam locomotives in the early days, there being a small locmotive shed provided here.

The Southport Fork, or avoiding line, enables trains to bypass Chapel Street station, though only special passenger trains do this, all normal service trains running into the station. Electric trains use the curve when proceeding to, or returning from Meols Cop Works but steam trains arriving at platforms 2 and 3 use the complete triangle in order to reverse, backing round towards Liverpool, reversing, then drawing forward over the avoiding line, whence a further reversal brings them into the station again with the locomotive leading ready for their next departure with passengers. There is another triangular layout nearby, which will be dealt with presently. Such track arrangements were generally favoured by the Lancashire & Yorkshire Railway Company and were to be found in several places which the system served, as a glance of a map of that busy line will confirm.

It is not often that a coal yard is located adjacent to a large terminal station, but this is actually the case at Southport. A small yard with a couple of sidings, almost hidden from the view of passengers is situated on the Down side of the station, the lead-in track curving sharply to the left immediately before the platform ramps are reached. Road vehicles enter this coal yard via a narrow passage leading from Tulketh Street, a thoroughfare which runs alongside the passenger station.

Great changes have been made at Southport Chapel Street station since 1963, which may be conveniently mentioned at this point in the story — other changes made along the line will be referred to later. A complete rebuilding project has swept away the old, weatherbeaten and obsolete L & Y edifice, which has been replaced by a new station that incorporates an office block and shopping precinct. The number of platforms has been reduced, numbers 1 to 6 being retained and the remainder filled-in and converted into a parking ground for motor vehicles. The London Street excursion platforms have also been abolished and the space used for a car park. Rebuilding was carried out with only slight interference to railway traffic, and was completed on 15th March, 1973, this being the "opening date" of the new station, though there was no "closing" date for the old one — transformation was gradual, the new image taking over from the old in a steady progressive work programme. The Victoria footbridge too has been replaced by a new concrete span.

It is unfortunately necessary to deal with the next section of the electrified lines in the past tense, as the Southport-Crossens service is now with the lost ages. The Crossens line was, in effect, a penetration of the third-rail into the suburbs at the Northern end of the town which was well developed for residential purposes early in the present century. The distance between Chapel Street and Crossens by rail was three miles, the running time being only 11 minutes. This section of railway was exposed to competition from bus services, and latterly was not very busy in off-peak hours, a situation that applied also to the buses. Three intermediate stations were served, these, with the exception of Meols Cop being also served by steam trains running between Southport and Preston.

The trains on the Crossens service made use of platform 9 at Chapel Street station, and were thus separated from the Liverpool trains. This arrangement avoided the necessity for them to cross several busy tracks to gain their own route, which would have been the case had they shared the extreme Down side platforms with the Liverpool service, though the existing track layout did not give any direct connections between platforms 1-3 and the line to Crossens. Normally the service was worked by three-car trains of the standard type, the original ex-L & Y "Orange Box" trains having been disposed of at the end of World War 2. Most of the trains called at Meols Cop and reversed direction at that station, but certain peak-hour trains proceeded direct to Crossens, taking the left-hand curve at Hawkshead Street Junction, the former East Lancashire Railway line to Wigan, traversed by Crossens trains as far as Meols Cop, continuing straight ahead. A triangular junction layout connected the Crossens and Preston line with that to Wigan, in the centre of which was situated the previously mentioned workshops which dealt with the servicing and partial overhaul of the electric rolling stock. The main building of this establishment was of red brick construction and architecturally was typical of the early electric traction era.

Major overhauls of rolling stock were not carried out at Meols Cop, so trains requiring such attention were (and still are) despatched to the main works at Horwich. When this is done the motor bogies are removed and replaced by diamond-frame wagon bogies for the journey to and from Horwich, the sets being hauled by a steam or diesel locomotive. While the set is away the motors and bogies are overhauled and replaced when the train returns, freshly painted and refurbished ready for a further spell of arduous service. Shunting of rolling stock at Meols Cop was usually performed by a spare motor unit. Until 1932 overhauls of the electric trains were carried out at Newton Heath carriage and wagon works, but these were closed down by the LMS company in that year, having become outdated and inadequate for their purpose.

On leaving Chapel Street station a train proceeding to Crossens passed the carriage sidings and steam motive power depot, the latter (which was closed in 1966) being on the Up side of the line to the left, quite near Chapel Street station approaches. A short run of three-quarters of a mile brought the train to St. Luke's station after passing St. Luke's Junction with its ex-L & Y signal box. Here the Wigan Direct line, opened in March, 1911 diverged on the right-hand side and passing through Blowick station, rejoined the older Wigan line at Pool Hey Junction on the outskirts of Southport. This latter line, together with Blowick station (which had an adjacent level crossing) was completely closed with effect from 12th June, 1965. It fulfilled a valuable role during the years the Chapel Street station dealt with a very heavy holiday traffic, now alas gone for ever so far as the railways are concerned — cars and motor coaches carry the crowds to Southport nowadays, a smaller proportion using the railway, which is still busy nevertheless.

St. Luke's was a rather small, timber-built station which had two widely separated island platforms, one on the original line, the other on the newer line. It was developed from the former West Lancashire Railway Company's Windsor Road Station (otherwise known as Ash Street) and the original St. Luke's, rebuilding into one station having taken place in June, 1902. Windsor Road station was closed on that date. St. Luke's station survived long after the Crossens and Preston train services had been abandoned, but was closed on 8th September, 1968. It was a rather gloomy edifice, with several sidings on its South side. The railway traverses an older residential district hereabouts and is almost at street level. Hawkshead Street Junction with its adjacent ex-L & Y signal box was reached beyond St. Luke's, the aforementioned curve to the left being the Crossens and Preston line, the electric train workshops being on its right-hand side. The line straight ahead presently reached the Easterly section of the triangular junction (after passing along the Southern side of the workshops) at Meols Cop Junction, controlled by an ex-L & Y signal box, and next came Meols Cop passenger station, another island platform structure at which the electric trains used the Up side. Here the driver and guard changed places due to the fact that the train reversed its direction of travel. Once more on its way, the train passed Meols Cop Junction again, but this time the right-hand curve was taken, with the workshops now on the left, to join the Preston line at Roe Lane Junction, with yet another ex-L & Y signal box to control its points and signals. The direct line from Hawkshead Street Junction to Roe Lane Junction was electrified in 1904 as part of the original scheme, the Meols Cop Junction-Roe Lane Junction curve not being so dealt with until 1909.

To revert to Meols Cop for a moment; the Wigan line divided a little distance Eastwards, at Butts Lane Junction, the track diverging to the right here becoming the Altcar & Hillhouse Branch, which was once a railway in its own right — the ponderously titled Liverpool, Southport & Preston Junction Railway which was later taken over by the L & Y.

Continuing beyond Roe Lane Junction the first station to be reached was Hesketh Park, approached through a residential area, the railway being in a shallow cuttings. This small station had brick and stone buildings. A small goods and coal yard was situated at the North end of the station on the Down side, which continued to be served for a little while after closure of the passenger station. Hesketh Park station opened on 19th February, 1878 took its name from the beautiful Park that was laid out on land that was once covered by sand dunes.

Leaving Hesketh Park, the track continued onto an embankment, soon reaching Churchtown, once a fishing village but now well inland owing to recession of the sea, and considerably developed for residential purposes. Churchtown station was situated on the embankment and was reached by stairs from the street below. The station platforms and building were of timber construction. Only passenger traffic was dealt with, there being no yard or sidings for goods. Beyond Churchtown the railway again reached road level,. descending on a gradient of 1 in 100 or so, this being the steepest section of track on the electrified lines. Runaway catch points were provided on the Up line on this steep incline.

Shallow earthen cuttings brought the line to Crossens, a residential and partly industrial district on the outskirts of Southport, fields and open countryside taking the place of streets and buildings beyond. Crossens station was rather small — a country station raised in importance but not altered. It was opened on 19th February, 1878. Of brick and stone construction, the station maintained its rural appearance and atmosphere in spite of being served by electric trains. From the main road a driveway gave access to the Down platform, whilst the Up platform was reached by a separate and much longer driveway. Between the extremities of these two drives the main road (Bankfield Lane) crossed the railway by an overbridge. An open footbridge linked the station's two platforms. There were several sidings situated to the North of the station on the Down side, and a loop on the Up side- which served a small engineering works. A carriage shed was provided North of the station, used for electric rolling stock, but this fell out of use for this purpose shortly before World War 2. During this war it was used for other purposes, but after hostilities had ceased, the shed was sold and the rails removed.

The electric trains from Southport, after all passengers had alighted, drew forward and then reversed on the trailing crossover provided for the purpose. They then either waited in a siding or returned immediately to Southport after taking on passengers from the Up platform. Beyond Crossens the non-electrified line continued onwards to Preston.

Crossens residents did not have a frequent train service until electrification, as prior to that event only trains running between Southport and Preston called at their station. In the late 1880's there were about a dozen trains in each direction on weekdays and half that number on Sundays. After the introduction of the electric trains the weekday service became a vastly improved one of about 52 trains each way — there was even a 20-minute service on Sundays after the 1.42 p.m. train the morning service being less frequent. In addition, trains to and from Preston called on both weekdays and Sundays. By the time of World War 2 the service consisted of about 52 trains each way on weekdays and 36 on Sundays. The Preston service provided additional trains.

In 1959 the Southport-Crossens service consisted of approximately 36 trains in each direction on weekdays, with trains to and from Preston also calling at Crossens. The electric train service was withdrawn on Sundays about this time, leaving Crossens to be served by six trains in each direction on the Preston line — back to the position as it was in the 1880's! In 1963 both the Crossens and Preston train services were listed for abandonment under the "Beeching Plan", and despite numerous protests, the closures were passed and the dreaded notices went up on the station hoardings. The prospect of an electric train service being abolished raised numerous eyebrows — there was not even any consideration given to the possibility of replacing the electric trains by diesel sets as had been proposed for the Ormskirk line when economies were in prospect, of which more later.

The night of Saturday, 5th September, 1964 saw the last electric train depart from Chapel Street for Crossens at 10.55 p.m., the flashes from its collector shoes on the soon to be de-energised live rail signalling a last farewell and the end of an era. From then on passengers travelled between Southport and Crossens on the buses, increases in the service being made to absorb the displaced rail travellers.

The steam train service between Southport and Preston came to an end the next evening — Sunday 6th September, when the last train, strengthened by three additional coaches to accommodate railway enthusiasts and members of the general public making sentimental journeys, departed in charge of 2-6-4 Tank locomotive No. 42296, and so followed the Crossens electric trains into oblivion. Few stations witnessed a double funeral as did Crossens, for this was its own end too, and when the red tail lamp of the Preston train had vanished into the night, the station gates were closed for the last time. There was to be no railway at all at Crossens shortly!

The echoes of the final train had hardly died away when the line was de-electrified with intense haste, dismantling of the permanent-way following with equal industry, but the work came to a halt a few days later, as Hesketh Park coal yard had to be kept open and so, the section between Roe Lane Junction and the coal yard lasted until 24th June, 1968. After that date the railway North of Roe Lane Junction ceased to exist, as track removal quickly followed. So passed into history the old West Lancashire Railway of rural charm, which became a suburban line for the first three miles out of Southport but remained rural for the remainder of its length until the outskirts of Preston were reached, at which it met the main line of Anglo-Scottish expresses and busy traffic.

The signalling on the Liverpool-Southport line, including the Crossens extension is mainly of the manually operated semaphore type except for the colour-light installations mentioned earlier. Almost all the former L & Y lower-quadrant semaphore signals had vanished by the early 1960's. The last L & Y signal at Southport Chapel Street was a bracket type with four posts, situated at the excursion platforms, which was still in existence in 1963, whilst the last one on the Liverpool line was the Down Slow line starting signal at Seaforth & Litherland station, which was replaced by an upper-quadrant signal in 1963.

97

Enthusiasts special train at Ormskirk on Saturday 4th October, 1980 – the last journey of the 1939 rolling stock. Note the connecting loop on the left, linking the Liverpool-Ormskirk line with that to Preston, now two separate railways.
(Photo: S.G. Jones)

View Northwards from Hall Road station, 1953. Sidings and repair shop for electric rolling stock on West side of main line. (Photo: J.W. Gahan)

*The electric rolling stock repair works at Meols Cop, photographed in 1968,
shortly before closure and demolition.* (Photo: J.W. Gahan)

*Kirkdale, 1985. View looking North showing Merseyrail electric train depot
tracks on the left, the two main running lines (centre) and on the right the site of
the former Wigan and Manchester line and in the distance the former Cheshire
Lines Railway tunnel portals. The CL lines (from Walton to Huskisson goods
depot) descended to a lower level here.* (Photo: S.G. Jones)

The Ormskirk Line

Having completed our exploration of the Southport line, we now return to Bank Hall, Bootle, to commence a survey of the railway Northwards to Ormskirk. This line is part of what started as the Liverpool, Ormskirk & Preston Railway, the Act for which was passed on 18th August, 1846. The line actually commenced at what became Walton Junction, at which it joined the Liverpool & Bury Railway. Construction of the LO & P began at Maghull on 16th March, 1847 and the line was completed early in 1849, being opened on 22nd April of that year. The Parliamentary Bill was opposed by the Liverpool & Manchester and North Union Railway Companies, which provided a roundabout route from Liverpool to Preston, but their opposition did not succeed. Engineers in charge of construction were Locke and Errington, the contractors being Brassey, McKenzie and Stephenson.

We must look at the Ormskirk line as it was up until the early 1960's because alterations carried out since that time have reduced the railway between Liverpool, Ormskirk and Preston to a mere skeleton of its former ample body. After passing the junction at Sandhills, at which the Southport lines diverge, the line goes beneath Stanley Road Bridge and immediately beyond lies the large Bank Hall steam Motive Power Depot with lines of engines standing in a smoky haze and overlooked by the high concrete coaling plant. An ex-L & Y signal box, Kirkdale West, controls movements here, whilst deep below in cutting and tunnels passes the ex-L & NWR line from Edge Hill to Canada and Alexandra Docks. To the right are extensive carriage sidings, and beyond the engine sheds on the left are further carriage sidings and cleaning depot. A rail-served scrap metal yard is also on this side of the line. To the right, at lower level, the Cheshire Lines Huskisson line plunges into tunnels beneath residential and industrial streets.

Kirkdale station, on the South side of the bridge carrying Hawthorne Road over the railway is a gloomy and war-blitzed two-platform brick structure with primitive brick waiting shelters, the platforms being reached via stairways from a covered footbridge. The electric lines pass through the station, whilst behind it on the East side are the "steam" lines from Wigan, Manchester etc. Immediately beyond the bridge is a deep cutting at the entrance to which is an ex-L & Y signal box, Kirkdale East. Next come two long tunnels separated by a short open stretch (once continuous tunnel) known as Kirkdale Nos. 1 and 2, and after a short length of cutting, near its end is located Walton Junction ex-L & Y signal box. Here the four-track section ends, to become two towards Preston and two for Wigan etc.

Beyond Walton Junction the Ormskirk line runs into an earthen cutting, a sudden change from the rocky gloom of Kirkdale tunnels and cuttings, and from here the line designations change, the Up line becoming the Down line and vice-versa. Only a little distance beyond the divergence is Walton Junction pasenger station, with its platforms in the cutting reached by sloping footpaths from the streets that are at a higher level than the railway. An overbridge beyond the station carries Hornby Road over the line, which continues in a wide earthen cutting and, only half-a-mile distant, reaches Orrell Park station, which was opened in 1906 in view of the heavy residential development in the district. Between the stations a plate-girder bridge spans the cutting, by means of which the ex-Midland Railway Fazakerley North Junction-Langton Dock goods line crosses over the L & Y line.

Orrell Park station is actually a glorified halt with a small timber shelter on either platform, and a ticket office situated on Orrell Lane overbridge that crosses the line at the North end of the platforms. Flights of steps give access for passengers. A little way South of the station, on the Up side of the line, is a very small ex-L & Y signal cabin bearing the title Orrell Park Box. This is manned during peak traffic times in order to shorten the rather long block section that extends from Walton Junction to Aintree, and enables extra traffic to be dealt with.

Onwards from Orrell Park the railway is still in a cutting, which continues until Aintree is approached, and is crossed by stone bridges carrying minor roads. The ex-Cheshire Lines Railway line from Hunts Cross to Southport passes below the L & Y line near Aintree, itself in a cutting, and then curves to run parallel with the latter through and beyond Aintree. Not far beyond this crossing of the two lines is another, the North Mersey Branch running from Fazakerley to the North Docks passing above on a high bridge. The Aintree Sorting Sidings East Cabin up on the embankment (an ex-L & Y signal box) controls the approaches to the vast marshalling yard that spreads over the land to the West, and adjacent to which is the large Aintree locomotive depot with its tall coaling plant tower looming large and prominent in the district. Aintree is a place of ceaseless activity, with trains and engines arriving and leaving at all times of the day and night.

Near Aintree passenger station the cutting ends, and a double-track line accompanied by several lengthy sidings curves in on the left-hand side, whilst the main line from Liverpool throws off two additional tracks, making a complex layout which is overlooked by the tall signal box which although a former L & Y edifice, is not of that company's standard design. Named Aintree Station Junction, the signal box stands on the Down side immediately South of Park Lane overbridge, which has recently been widened, as the road was extremely narrow where it passed over the railway. The passenger station, through which four sets of rails pass, consists of two side platforms and an island, of which only the Down platform and Up face of the island are in regular daily use, the others being utilised only on days when racing is being held, as the station is situated close to the famous Aintree racecourse at which the "Grand National" is run. An extensive awning covers much of the Down platform, this having been added when improvements were carried out to the station in 1912. The island platform has only a small timber waiting room, but the Up side platform has no shelter of any kind, as it sees only occasional use.

The station booking office is at roadway level on the bridge, whilst an open footbridge connects the platforms, this being immediately adjacent to the road bridge, the two being side-by-side. At the rear of the Down platform there is a small goods and coal yard with several sidings, part of which was used to make a turning circle for buses after the Aintree tram route was abandoned. Other sidings for stabling electric trains are situated to the North of the station. The track on the West side of the island platform was used on "Grand National" day by trains of the Liverpool Overhead Railway, which provided a special race day service between Dingle and Aintree, the last occasion being in 1956, as the LOR was closed at the end of that year.

The ex-CLC line mentioned earlier continued alongside the L & Y line for some considerable distance beyond Aintree, but was cut back to the latter place for passenger traffic in 1952. A crossover connection between the two railways is provided North of Aintree station, controlled by an ex-L & Y signal box named Aintree C-L-C Junction (the hyphens are actually included) situated on the Up side of the L & Y line. The importance of this junction has declined in recent years and it sees little traffic nowadays.

Immediately beyond Aintree station the four sets of rails merge into two again and the railway runs onto a fairly high embankment. On the Down side there are several short sidings, whilst a single track branch line diverges in a North-easterly direction, curving to pass over Ormskirk Road on a plate-girder bridge, then enters the extensive grounds of the British Enka rayon factory, which was established here in 1926. Recent road widening necessitated lengthening of this bridge, but shortly after this had been done the factory ceased to make use of rail transport! Several "Fireless" steam locomotives were used around the works and hauled wagons to and from the exchange sidings. A number of old wooden mineral wagons which formerly belonged to collieries were used for internal working in the factory, still in their original but well weathered colour schemes, but bearing the title of BRITISH ENKA in fresh white lettering.

The ex-CLC line runs parallel on the West side of the L & Y line, both lines on embankments, but the former ends just short of Old Roan, a place named after a nearby inn. Both lines crossed the B5194 road on bridges, but the CLC bridge has been demolished and little trace of the line onwards towards Southport remains to be seen. The CLC did not have a station at Old Roan, but the LMS company built one here in 1935 in order to serve the developing residential district. The suburbs are creeping further and further Northwards, new housing spreading over the fields in an almost continuous process, whilst former country roads are being turned into main arteries teeming with traffic. Immediately before Old Roan station is reached the line crosses the Leeds & Liverpool Canal for the second time after leaving Exchange, and as already mentioned, crosses also the B5194 road, the station being situated up on the embankment on the North side of the roadway. In similar fashion to many other suburban stations of the 1930's, simple timber platforms and waiting shelters are provided, with none of the elaborate facilities of earlier stations.

As the railway continues Northwards two further bridges are crossed, a lengthy plate-girder structure and an old stone arch bridge spanning new and old roadways, whilst a third but smaller bridge spans the narrow River Alt. The countryside is still quite rural for the next few miles, but residential and industrial development is taking place here and there in the area. From the high embankment extensive views are obtained of fields and woods, with the skyline of Liverpool in the distance. Proceeding onwards the embankment gradually peters out and the railway assumes the level of the surrounding land, passing over the Leeds & Liverpool Canal yet again, and a level crossing immediately before entering Maghull station. This was once a rural country station with little habitation nearby, but is now on the fringe of a fair-sized town which has developed largely since the end of the 1939 war. The level crossing is controlled by an ex-L & Y signal box, which is on the Down side on the South side of the roadway.

Notwithstanding the fact that Maghull station has for very many years been situated on an electrified line, it has managed to keep its "country" character, and is in a pleasant situation. The industrial and residential development of recent years has not affected the railway to a very great extent and only moderate numbers of passengers use the trains except at peak hours, although the future looks brighter in this respect. On the Up side of the line at the rear of the station there is a small goods and coal yard with several sidings.

Between Maghull and the following station which is that of Town Green & Aughton, the railway passes through partly wooded countryside in shallow cuttings, then runs onto an embankment again. Town Green station has sidings either side of the main line, and a small goods and coal yard with sidings on the Down side. One of the sidings is used by the Royal Train on occasions when Royal Persons visit Knowsley Hall, whilst one of the Up side sidings is electrified but sees little use for electric trains, which are usually stabled at Ormskirk. Some of these sidings have however, been removed in recent times. The signal box which is on the Up side is a recently constructed brick and concrete building situated to the South of the station and replaced a former ex-L & Y box which stood well back from the line in a clearing in the trees on the Down side of the line, and was in a truly idyllic location.

Town Green is typical of L & Y country stations, with platforms and buildings of brick and stone, with approach roads on either side. Pleasant gardens are a beautifying feature here, as indeed they are at many such stations throughout the land, but are a vanishing facet of the railway scene with so many closures of country stations taking place. Station garden competitions, once so common and popular, are likely to see fewer entries as time passes and the rural stations disappear.

After passing through an earthen cutting with grassy banks crossed by old stone bridges, we reach Aughton Park station, a small modernistic one situated in a rock cutting. This station was built in 1913 to serve a developing residential district. Previously there was a simple halt here, with no platforms, and was served by a steam rail motor which had folding steps. Stairways lead up to the roadway above the cutting. Beyond the station, on the up side, is the stone quarry operated by Joseph Crook & Sons, served by a loop line, which however fell out of use in 1961. The product of the quarry was, for many years, despatched in red-liveried open wagons with the owner's name boldly lettered in white, and were a pleasant sight in latter days when few privately owned railway wagons remained. These wagons too, disappeared in 1961 and for some months the stone was conveyed in BR steel roadstone wagons. By the end of that year however, the quarry ceased to be rail-served and the loop line became hidden under long grass. To be futuristic for a moment, the quarry was closed in 1968 and the loop rails were removed, although the points at each end were left in place until the next relaying job.

A sand quarry was once worked on the Down side of the railway, served by a siding and a signal box. Its site was approximately that on which Aughton Park station now stands. The quarry was disused by 1909 however, and the siding box subsequently removed.

Deep cuttings with steep rocks walls and bridges built in yellow sandstone are features of the line as it approaches Ormskirk, the rock giving way to grass-covered slopes with stone retaining walls nearer the town. Eventually the land to the left opens out wider and two long sidings are provided here for stabling empty passenger coaches between runs. They were also used by trains on the Ormskirk-Southport service, a train, complete with locomotive standing by until departure time drew near, when it would move ahead into the station, load up and be smartly on its way within minutes. Both local and long-distance trains used the main-line platforms, as no bay or loop was provided for steam trains except for a short bay for the Rainford Junction trains. The Southport service ceased on 4th March, 1962, and as there were no local Ormskirk-Preston trains by that time, the sidings became disused and rusty. An air of desolation became apparent, because the Southport train, with its sizzling 2-6-4 Tank locomotive had become such a familiar and homely sight over the years that its loss was very real.

Ormskirk is 12¼ miles from Liverpool by rail, and the station is still a busy one in spite of train withdrawals as, in addition to the local electric trains, all those between Liverpool and Preston stop there including most of the long distance trains. Only the electric trains call at the intermediate stations between Ormskirk and Liverpool so that any passenger coming from the North destined for say Maghull, changes to an electric train for the last portion of the journey. The importance of this junction station has however, considerably declined since the cessation of the Southport and Rainford Junction services.

Ormskirk station has two main platforms, a long extension of the Down platform at its South end forming a bay which is the terminus for the majority of the electric trains. As the station is situated below the level of the main road, the latter crosses the railway on a stone bridge at the South end. A sloping approach road on the East side permits entry and exit for passengers and vehicles. A small yard fronts the main station building which is also on the East side, this building being of brick and stone construction and probably dates from the time the railway was built. A commodious brick open-fronted shelter provides accommodation on the West side, whilst both platforms are partially covered by awnings. An open footbridge connects both platforms, and the station has a bookstall, the only one between Liverpool and Preston with such a useful facility. The station presents a pleasant, old-world appearance being situated in an older part of the town. At the North end of the East platform the bay for the Rainford Junction trains was situated, and alongside this was a small coaling stage for the locomotives used on that run.

A small coal yard with sidings is situated on the East side at the North end of Ormskirk station, whilst a fairly large goods yard with several sidings lies to the rear of the Up platform towards its Northern end. The large ex-L & Y signal box is the most prominent feature of the Up platform, on which it stands at the Northern extremity. This box controls the whole of the station and sidings, together with the Rainford Branch junction, the latter branch curving to the right, passing round the back of the town and vanishing into a tree-shaded cutting. Rainford Branch Sidings signal box, of standard L & Y design can be seen in the middle distance.

105

To the North of Ormskirk there are several long sidings on the East side of the main line, some of which are used for stabling electric trains. A train, upon completing its scheduled period of service, runs into the Up main line platform instead of the bay, and after its passengers have alighted, proceeds to one of the sidings to await its next turn of duty, when the process is reversed, the train departing for Liverpool from the Down main platform. Finally, there remains to be mentioned the cattle dock with its siding at the South end of the Up platform. For a small "country town" station Ormskirk has quite a lot of facilities — there was even an engine shed until 1936.

The forgoing describes the Liverpool-Ormskirk line as it was until about the middle 1960's, when economies began to be made in various directions. From 1969 however, the axe has been wielded with energy and vigour over the whole line between Kirkdale and Preston, reducing the once busy railway to a mere skeleton. Although the local electric train service has improved, goods traffic has virtually disappeared, and there is none at all North of Aintree, whilst the Liverpool-Preston passenger service has been cut back to Ormskirk and worked by diesel MU trains on a line that has been largely singled North of Ormskirk. No longer is the latter station a busy centre for rail traffic, for all sidings and other tracks have been removed. Even the electric trains are stabled elsewhere today, but for some years one set remained overnight on the previously mentioned electrified siding at Town Green. Even the "electric bay" has been abolished, and quite remarkable terminal arrangements were instituted in May, 1970. The only track now normally used at Ormskirk station is the former Down main line, and mid-way along the platform this has been broken for a few yards, with two sets of buffer stop-blocks erected so that electric trains arriving from Liverpool and diesel trains from Preston, which now use the same platform, are kept safely apart! In case it should ever be required to run a train through from Liverpool to Preston or vice-versa, a part of the former Up main line has been retained in the form of a loop. It came in useful however, on Sunday 1st October, 1972 when train diversions were put in force due to the phasing-in of the Warrington power signal box. On that day three passenger trains from Liverpool Lime Street, the 8.52 a.m. to Blackburn, 10.50 a.m. to Blackpool and 4.35 p.m. to Glasgow were routed via the Bootle Branch, onto the Southport line at Bootle Junction, from whence they proceeded via Marsh Lane Junction and through to Aintree via the North Mersey Branch. From Aintree the trains ran forward to Ormskirk, where they by-passed the stop blocks and headed North for Preston — the first main line trains to use the line since May, 1970. Other such workings have since occured, including movements in the reverse direction, but they have been few and far between.

The large and once very busy signal box at Ormskirk station has been demolished, and those signals that still remain are controlled by

Town Green box. It is the absence of the once numerous semaphore signals that gives Ormskirk station such an air of desertion today, as there was a large number in the vicinity. Altogether, the railway scene at this once lively station is a depressing one, the thought of trains passing through in each direction every few minutes, also Scottish expresses and goods trains seems to savour of fantasy! In all probability goods trains are unlikely to ever be seen again at Ormskirk. The town itself is gradually losing its old-time atmosphere through redevelopment and expansion, whilst its population has greatly increased. In spite of these factors it still seems remote from Liverpool, whilst the local dialect is distinct from that of Liverpolitans, and is hard to realise that a train ride of only 28 minutes duration separates this market town from the enormous city on the River Mersey shore, only 12 miles distant.

Apart from the removal of rails in the vicinity of Ormskirk station, the air of desolation is made even more apparent by the absence of roling stock where previously many carriages and wagons formed part of the daily scene. Even the trains that still serve the station are shortened versions of those employed in former times, except during peak traffic periods. Elsewhere along the line closures and track removals have taken place — at Aintree, where the goods sidings have gone, the same thing happening also at Maghull, in 1964. Again, signal boxes have been reduced in number and the only ones left after 1970 were Kirkdale East, Walton Junction, Aintree Station Junction, Maghull, and Town Green. Indeed, if it had not been for the existence of the level crossing Maghull box might have gone also, but it still survives in spite of the crossing gates being replaced by lifting barriers in July, 1977. Kirkdale East box was closed in 1977 when the underground Link Line was opened and the signals worked from James Street new power signal box. It was latterly designated Sandhills No. 2.

The scene at Aintree is as desolate today as that at Ormskirk. Only the Up and Down Liverpool lines pass through the main platforms, whilst a single line leading to Sefton Junction trails off the Up line on the Liverpool side of Park Lane bridge. From this runs a single track siding which becomes a long loop passing behind the station on its West side, with a single connection to a couple of sidings that are the last remnant of the former Cheshire Lines Railway Hunts Cross-Southport line. These sidings serve industrial plants to the North of Aintree station, but see little traffic nowadays. The large Aintree Station Junction signal box still remains, but is opened only when required. It works a few remaining points — there are no signals whatever at Aintree now.

West of Aintree the North Mersey Branch has been closed beyond North Mersey Branch Junction, whilst the vast Aintree Sorting Sidings were closed, due mainly to the decline of the docks, whilst spur lines serving several industrial premises have also been abandoned, all these lines ceasing to be used after 1964. Removal of the sorting sidings left acres of empty land, but fortunately freight traffic has returned in some measure by the establishment of a rail-served container base on the site of the former West End Sidings, near Ford. Presence of the GIRO headquarters raises hopes of revived passenger train services along the remaining section of the North Mersey Branch at some future date.

All the passenger stations between Liverpool and Ormskirk have undergone modification and improvement over the years, including replacement of gas lighting by electric illumination. However, Walton Junction and Ormskirk still had gas lamps as late as 1968, even though the line had been electrified for more than half a century! Indeed, gas lighting died hard, and even the city of Liverpool still had a large number of gas lamps is use until 1970.

In 1964 there was a scheme afoot to abandon electric traction on the Ormskirk line, with the possibility of the same thing happening on the Southport line also, when the equipment became due for renewal, and replacement of the electric trains by diesel train sets. Apart from the matter of reliability in which the electric trains are vastly superior to the diesel units, such a move would not necessarily have been a detracting factor on the Ormskirk service as it was then, as it seemed to be within the capacity of diesel traction to handle, but had the use of diesels been ever actually extended to the Southport line with its heavy loading, high speeds and traffic demands requiring a high degree of reliability, the results might not have been so good. The electric trains have proved over many years to be entirely reliable and complete masters of their onerous work, fully capable of meeting any demands made upon them. Any other form of traction on the Southport line could only be regarded as a serious step backwards.

The electrification of the Liverpool-London main line on the 25kv overhead catenary system instead of using a live rail tended to make the older established electric railways on Merseyside seem somewhat outdated, but overhead wire electrification (though not on 25kv) is almost as old as the live rail system, but as part of the propaganda build-up for conversion to diesel operation, it was preached by BR that the third-rail system had become obsolete. Nevertheless, the Southern Region of British Railways was, in the late 1960's, engaged on extending its already vast third-rail electrification over the main line to Southampton and Bournemouth, whilst other main line schemes on the Region had been completed in recent times. The third-rail system is however, perfectly suited to passenger carrying lines and its reliability needs no emphasis, the exemplary service of such electrification on the enormously trafficked Southern system being proof enough of its practicability, though it may be less economical than the 25kv system. After the Southern Region had completed the Bournmouth electrification scheme they introduced a periodical newsletter to passengers entitled "Third Rail", proving that the authorities down South did not share their Northern colleague's disdain for live rails! Even had the Southport and Ormskirk lines been converted to diesel however, the Wirral lines would still have displayed their third-rails to embarrass the Public Relations people!

As part of the economy campaign of the early 1960's it was proposed to withdraw Sunday trains on the Liverpool-Ormskirk line, but after many protests had been voiced, this action was not carried out. It is only fair to add however, that the line is exposed to intense competition from buses and private cars, but so far as running times are concerned, the trains are vastly superior. Even the mighty bus has to fight the car for passengers nowadays, just as the train had to fight the bus for years! Co-ordination came later.

The proposal to convert the Ormskirk line to diesel operation was eventually dropped and the electric trains continued in use. Some Sunday journeys were turned over to diesel however, and the last evening train from Liverpool on weekdays was sometimes a diesel set for a time. Such sets were used on both the Ormskirk and Southport lines during the coal miner's strike in the snowy February of 1972, interspersed with electric trains, and although at that time the diesels were acclaimed because they had heating whereas the heat was turned off on the electric trains to save current, few people want to see diesel trains regularly. Rather, everyone looked forward to a new fleet of electric trains to replace the ageing stalwarts which were still at work in the late 1970's after countless thousands of miles of shuttling to and fro on their busy tasks.

A multiple-unit train with control trailer car No. 3051, photographed at Meols Cop in L&Y days. (Photo: K. Longbottom collection)

Near the end of its days. An ex-L&Y train photographed early in the 1939 war. The leading car has had its body strengthened with vertical strips. A new LMS train is in the background. (Photo: K. Longbottom collection)

Station and train staff pose with one of the then new electric trains at Southport, Chapel Street circa. 1904. (Photo: F. Dean collection)

Train Services Ormskirk Line

Train services between Liverpool Exchange and Ormskirk were not very frequent in pre-electric days, the latter place being served only by trains running between Liverpool and Preston, also between Liverpool and Southport via Burscough Junction. After electrification Aintree and Maghull enjoyed a very frequent service of about 56 trains in each direction on weekdays and 18 on Sundays, Ormskirk did not receive the benefit of these frequent trains until the electrification reached the town. For some time Aintree and Maghull were served by alternate trains, most of those to Aintree running via Kirkdale and the majority of the Maghull trains travelling via Bootle, Marsh Lane Junction and the North Mersey Branch, joining the main line at Aintree.

In 1910 about 19 steam trains in each direction served Ormskirk on weekdays but only six on Sundays, all these being Southport or Preston trains. There was also however, a service provided by a steam rail motor between Maghull and Ormskirk, making 16 return trips on weekdays and eight on Sundays. One rail motor trip was extended to Aintree on Mondays-Saturdays, departing from Maghull at 6.11 p.m. and returning from Aintree at 6.20 p.m. As the line was already electrified as far as Maghull the rail motor seemed to defy progress — a "country branch" train in suburbia! The rail motors departed from the scene upon completion of electrification through to Ormskirk in 1913, but they continued to meet electric trains at the latter place for many more years because they were used on the local **Ormskirk-**Southport service and also on that to Rainford Junction. When Ormskirk was finally electrified it became the only market town in Britain to be situated on an electric railway.

Over the years the Liverpool-Ormskirk service was maintained on a frequent basis, but was not developed. In 1939 the service (via Kirkdale) consisted of about 40 trains in each direction on weekdays and 18 on Sundays. There were also a number of short workings to and from Aintree. Many of the steam trains between Liverpool and Preston also called at Ormskirk. By 1959 the service consisted of about 44 trains in each direction on weekdays and 25 on Sundays, augmented by the Preston trains.

The Liverpool-Ormskirk electric train service survived all threats and now seems likely to remain as part of the MERSEYRAIL system. The weekday service in 1972 consisted of approximately 40 trains in each direction, and 23 on Sundays, so it will be seen that the cutting down had ceased, but the service was not yet a regular-interval one as has almost always been the case on the Southport line. Commencing on 7th May, 1973 however, the Ormskirk line at last got a 20-minute regular-interval service on weekdays, outside peak periods during which it was augmented, and on Sundays a 30-minute service was provided for most of the day. Like Southport line passengers, those travelling to or from Ormskirk no longer needed to consult a timetable, except for early morning or late evening journeys. Further changes were made in 1977 when the underground Link Line was opened.

An ex-L&Y four-car electric train passing beneath the Cheshire Lines bridge near Woodvale in early LMS days. The line on the extreme right is Marshall's Siding. (Photo: J. Ward collection)

Liverpool-bound train at Blundellsands & Crosby station in L&Y days. The two leading cars are of the later domed roof type with metal panelling.
(Photo: J. Ryan collection)

A train of L&Y "Dingle Cars" at Maghull station before the electrification through to Ormskirk had been completed. (Photo: J. Ward collection)

The North Mersey Branch

The North Mersey Branch was originally conceived as a goods line running from Fazakerley to Bootle to serve the North Docks. The Act for its construction was passed on 17th May, 1861. Some quite heavy engineering works in the way of embankments, cuttings and bridges were involved, with an arched viaduct at Seaforth Sands. The line was opened on 27th August, 1866 and passed through an expanding industrial area at the Bootle end but more (then) rural country at its Eastern extremity where it joined the main line from Liverpool Exchange — Wigan, Manchester etc. Goods traffic only was operated until 1906. The branch was electrified between Aintree and Marsh Lane Junction, joining the Liverpool-Southport line at that junction. Stations were provided at Ford and Linacre Road, and passenger train service between Liverpool Exchange and Aintree by this route commenced on 1st June, 1906.

Ford station (the name of the district was derived from the existence of a ford on Rimrose Brook) was on the East side of Captains Lane overbridge adjacent to the West end of Aintree Sorting Sidings. Linacre Road station was, by contrast on an embankment, on the North-East side of the bridge that spans the thoroughfare from which it took its name. Both stations were simple in design, being glorified halts with timber buildings and platforms of the same material. They were a far cry from the grand and spacious stations of earlier times!

In 1914 the line was further electrified from North Mersey Branch Junction to the top of the North Mersey incline at Seaforth Sands, and a platform was provided for dock employees. This small halt station was named Gladstone Dock, its exact location being at the summit of the incline almost adjacent to the Seaforth Sands station of the Liverpool Overhead Railway. It consisted of only the one platform. A train service between Aintree and Gladstone was introduced on 7th September, 1914, with seven trains in each direction on weekdays and an extra each way on Saturdays. It was a useful facility for the dock workers during the Great War, but the numbers of passengers declined when peace returned and therefore the service was discontinued on 7th July, 1924. The "Dingle Cars" were used on the Gladstone Dock service rather than the large standard trains.

At the time of the outbreak of the first World War in 1914 a service of about 17 trains each way on weekdays was provided between Liverpool Exchange and Maghull via Marsh Lane, though a few trains terminated at Aintree. The were nine trains in each direction on Sundays. By the time of the second World War in 1939, approximately 29 trains were provided in each direction on Weekdays, to and from Aintree only. There was no Sunday service by this time. The war years and afterwards saw a gradual decline in the train service, and by 1951 it had become almost useless, as at that time there were only five trains in each direction Monday-Friday and four only on Saturdays, and as might have been expected the service was placed on the abandonment list. Nobody seems to have considered revitalising the service, which might well have regained ground as the line passes through a heavily populated and also industrial area, and so, on Saturday, 1st April, 1951 the trains were withdrawn, without ceremony — indeed, the service just faded away. No track abandonment was involved, and the line continued to be used for empty stock movements of electric trains for some years afterwards. Eventually the live rails were removed rendering the line inaccessible to electric trains.

A short-lived train service which used part of the North Mersey Branch was that between Aintree and Dingle via the Liverpool Overhead Railway. In 1906 a crossover was put in between the LOR and North Mersey line a little distance to the East of Seaforth Sands "overhead" station, and an L & Y signal box designated Rimrose Road Junction was built to control train movements. The service, worked by the "Dingle Cars" commenced in the year 1906 but was not a financial success, so it was discontinued in September, 1908. Another service run by the L & Y Company over the LOR system was that between Dingle and Southport, which commenced in 1906 but was withdrawn in August, 1914 as it was a loss-making operation. The "Dingle Cars" also operated this service, as the standard L & Y electric trains were too heavy, and the cars too long to allow them over the elevated structure of the overhead system. Passengers to and from stations on the latter railway going to, or coming from, Southport could change trains at Seaforth & Litherland after cessation of the through service, and this facility lasted until closure of the Liverpool Overhead Railway on 30th December, 1956.

Three-car set of 1927 Compartment stock at Aintree, with the steam locomotive shed in the background. These trains were known to the staff as the "Lindberghs". The motor coach is No. 28306.   (Photo: G. Sarson)

Driving trailer M29108M and unidentified motor coach in use for parcels, fish and mail traffic, seen on the servicing pit at Southport Chapel Street station in 1959. These are demoted 1927 compartment type vehicles withdrawn from passenger service.   (Photo: R. Stephens)

Adventures with the Elements

Although the Merseyside electrified lines are situated in an area that rarely sees extremes in weather conditions, nature has caused disruption and delay to train services on occasions. Heavy thunderstorms have caused flooding, mainly in the cutting near Waterloo, to a depth sufficient to submerge traction motors, and steam trains, with a variety of locomotives hauling them have been used until the waters subsided. Snow is, of course, the worst enemy of the railway and during the great and prolonged blizzards of January and February of the wartime year of 1940 the country's railways and roads were badly affected.

Saturday 28th January of that memorable year saw snow falling heavily in the evening, but trains kept running reasonably well, but next day, Sunday, the 12.05 p.m. train (an old L & Y set) from Southport to Liverpool, running late, became snowbound in a high drift near Roys Crossing between Hillside and Ainsdale, at 1.15 p.m. long after it should have been in Liverpool. A steam locomotive was despatched from Southport to try and push the train through but this ran into a drift that stopped any further progress a quarter of a mile short of its objective. About 20 passengers thereupon alighted in the snow and were cared-for by local residents, as the prospects of immediate alternative transport were nil. In the opposite direction there was no service between Liverpool and Southport from 11.15 a.m. until 5.00 p.m., when a few steam trains were operated. The Up line was cleared later in the day but the 8.35 p.m. from Birkdale to Liverpool, a steam train, became snowbound near Formby power station. Two steam locomotives were sent to assist but their combined efforts could not move the trapped train. Indeed, one of coaches was derailed in the attempt, and about 80 passengers were marooned in the train until 9.20 a.m. next morning, when they were taken back to Formby station on the 3.20 a.m. mail train from Liverpool which was running six hours late. Their journey to Liverpool was resumed on a special train which left Formby at 10.00 a.m.

On that never-to-be-forgotten weekend the Up line was blocked by the derailed coach from 9.00 p.m. on the Sunday until 1.30 p.m. on the Tuesday following, single line working having to be put into operation. Meanwhile troops and railwaymen worked in the driving snow and bitter cold to clear the lines. For days afterwards, steam locomotives hauled the electric trains. That terrible Winter of 1940 is still a vivid memory to those who experienced its rigours, as it was coupled with war conditions such as blackout at night, food and fuel shortages and so on.

More recent snows have caused some dislocation to electric train services, mostly through blocked points, but nothing on the scale of the 1940 onslaught by the "white fiend" has been experienced since, though 1947 posed some problems with its blizzards.

Periods of severe frost have caused difficulties through ice forming on conductor rails during the night hours, and when conditions have been really bad in the past a train has been run to and fro to keep the live rails clear. The L & Y electric trains had ice scrapers fitted to the bogies of certain cars which helped in this respect but they were not fitted to the later LMS trains. Brilliant displays of arcing are a feature of icy Winter weather on electric railways, accompanied by fizzing and spluttering from the collector shoes. Nowadays anti-freeze fluid is applied to the conductor rails.

Thunderstorms accompanied by torrential rain have proved troublesome in the past, and one such storm in July, 1945 caused flooding in the cutting at Waterloo to a depth that precluded the operation of electric trains due to their motors being vulnerable to water penetration. A service of steam trains running at 20-minute intervals was therefore provided between Liverpool Exchange and Hall Road, the electric trains running between the latter station and Southport. Locomotives employed on this emergency service were ex-L & Y 0-6-0, LMS Class 2P 4-4-0, Standard Compound 4-4-0, Hughes 2-6-0 and Standard Class 5 4-6-0. Tender-first running was involved in one direction, as of course, there were no turning facilities for steam locomotives at Hall Road. That normally quiet station became a busy hive of activity with all the shunting necessary to turn the steam trains for the return journeys to Liverpool.

Southport line Baggage Car M28497 in the scrap yard at Stanley, Liverpool.
June, 1966.   (Photo: J.W. Gahan)

Freight Traffic & Special Trains

We now come to the subject of goods traffic over the ex-L & Y Merseyside electrified lines, commencing with the Southport line. Even in the heydey of railways, goods trains were seldom seen by passengers once their trains were North of Seaforth, as not only was merchandise traffic light in comparison with that on other lines in the Merseyside area, but it was mostly dealt with during the night hours. Much agricultural produce was carried in earlier times, but road transport gradually acquired this traffic, leaving coal and general goods to the railway right up to, and during World War 2. An engine from Liverpool made its way from station to station as far as Hall Road, delivering loaded wagons and taking away the empties (and any that might have been loaded), and another engine, from Southport did likewise, working as far as Hightown. Other engines dealt with the local domestic coal traffic, working late into the evening. During World War 2 however, there were additional workings owing to the heavy volume of war traffic and on many occasions two engines were at work during the day time. After the end of the war however, general goods traffic dwindled away leaving only coal, but with the policy of closing local coal yards and replacing them with central bulk fuel depots, this traffic also came to an end at the local stations.

As a consequence of the run-down of freight traffic on the Southport and Ormskirk lines in the early 1960's, removal of sidings began to take place. In 1962 the large goods and coal yard at Seaforth was closed, followed in March, 1964 by removal of the Down side sidings at Birkdale, whilse those on the opposite side of the main line there were taken up in 1967. All sidings at Crosby were removed in 1966 leaving much empty land on both sides of the line. The long loop line known as Barkfield Siding which stretched from Formby to Freshfield was reduced to two short sidings, used as head-shunts for the remaining yards at those two places until 1967. Ainsdale yard closed on 28th November, 1966. The yards at Waterloo and Formby were closed in November, 1967, as also was the last remaining siding at Freshfield. Sniggery Siding at Hightown ceased to be used during 1967 also, leaving Marsh Lane as the only rail served coal depot on the whole of the Southport line. This yard was however, closed in May, 1973, a small housing estate now having obliterated the site.

As already noted, the goods and coal yards were shunted by steam locomotives working along the line progressively. The empty wagons collected from the yards at the Liverpool end of the line were usually left overnight in the long siding at Crosby, and worked away the following morning. The work of shunting began in the evening after the rush period was over, and continued until the task was completed. On Saturdays the work was done during the morning.

In LMS days the locomotives employed for goods and coal trips along the Southport line were the time-honoured L & Y 0-6-0's, occasionally being replaced by the large 0-8-0's of ex-L & Y or LMS Standard types. After the formation of British Railways the ex-L & Y engines took a diminishing share of the work, being gradually replaced by the small Ivatt 2-6-0's, or the older and much larger Horwich design 2-6-0's. The ex-War Department 2-8-0's also took a hand at times. The engines were usually provided by Aintree motive power depot. The same methods of working also applied to the Ormskirk line. Mention of the Southport line shunter produces a mental vision of a small engine such as an L & Y 0-6-0 puffing to and fro on its task, with the vacuum ejector sizzling continuously, a sound that identified these engines readily even if not in sight of the observer. The clashing of wagon buffers and rumble of drawgear provided their accompaniment, and the local populace knew that their fuel supplies were safely delivered, even if they were inclined to grumble at the noise. It was a friendly noise, however!

During 1965 changes began to be made in the time-honoured customs, and the engine employed on the coal yard shunting at the Liverpool end of the line was provided from Edge Hill, usually a Class 8F 2-8-0 which worked the yards at Marsh Lane and Waterloo. It left Edge Hill shed about 3.30 p.m. and travelled to Marsh Lane via the Bootle Branch and Bootle Junction. Upon completion of its work the engine brought the empty wagons to Stanley, on the Bootle Branch, where it left them for forwarding to the colliery next morning, and proceeded back to the shed, after which it worked the 11.00 p.m. express freight train from Edge Hill to Carnforth, retracing its path along the Bootle Branch and leaving Liverpool via Marsh Lane Junction and Aintree. This train was re-routed via Wigan in 1966, but a steam engine continued to be provided by Edge Hill for the shunting until early in May, 1968, when a diesel-electric locomotive, usually an English Electric Class 40 or Sulzer Class 24 took over the job.

The engine at the Southport end of the line was also a steam machine until 1966. On 12th April that year a 2-6-4 Tank, No. 42665 was unusally employed on the coal yard shunt. When steam finished, the work was handed over to a 350 hp diesel-electric 0-6-0 of Class 08, but by that time the remaining coal yards had not long to live.

Apart from the local coal yard shunters and the London-Southport through coach workings there were few steam locomotives seen on the line beyond Marsh Lane Junction. Prior to the last war however, all kinds of interesting engines appeared on excursion trains to North Wales and elsewhere, leaving the Southport line at Bootle Junction in order to traverse the ex-L & NWR Bootle Branch, over which they ran to Edge Lane Junction, thence to their various destinations. There were also excursions to

Southport and Blackpool from Bootle Branch stations. Alas, such excursions ended with the war, for ever. Many special trains for service personnel, also special freight trains operated over the Liverpool-Southport line during the war, some of them travelling very long distances, Electric trains were kept busy too, running between Hall Road and Bootle, also Aintree and Bootle during 1941-43 taking hundreds of troops to nightly duties along the docks, from camps at Crosby, Aintree etc.

An interesting example of a long-distance forces train originating on the Liverpool-Southport line was one that made the long journey from Hall Road to Pembroke in far-away West Wales on a cold, dark night in November, 1942. This consisted of L & NER corridor coaches and two LMS six-wheeled passenger brake vans, and was hauled by Class 5 4-6-0 No. 5045 of Edge Hill shed, being replaced by another engine at Shrewsbury. The train left the Southport line via Southport South Junction and St. Luke's, and took the direct line to Wigan, at which it gained the West Coast main line, proceeding thence to Crewe and onwards. The soldiery who bade good-bye to the wartime delights of Liverpool so sadly, found themselves in a vastly different location next morning when the train pulled up in the dawn light at the single platform of Pembroke station, with a Great Western engine — No. 4984 "Albrighton Hall" at the head.

Other steam workings noted along the Southport line during 1942 were as follows: Class 5XP 4-6-0 No. 5532 "Illustrious" hauled a forces train towards Liverpool in the early morning of 13th July. On Sunday, 19th July following, a special freight train ran, also in the early hours of the morning. On 27th August, Compound 4-4-0 No. 1186 travelled Northwards with empty passenger coaches in the morning, whilst on 25th September Class 5 4-6-0 No. 5436 (of Carlisle) hauled a forces train towards Liverpool in the evening. Most unusually, Class 2P 4-4-0 No. 691 hauled a freight train towards Southport at Mid-day on 15th October. There were many other steam workings of course, in those difficult days.

Perhaps not so unusual but nonetheless interesting, was the sight of one of the ex-L & Y baggage cars hauling a horse-box towards Liverpool on 30th September, 1942, providing some variety in the otherwise highly standarised service. When traffic was extra-heavy the baggage cars could, and sometimes did, haul an extra van or two, but they had to be vacuum brake-fitted vehicles of course.

During the years that Formby power station was working, coal supplies needed to be brought in, and the large quantities of ash and clinker taken away. After the Grouping ex-L & Y engines on power station runs were sometimes replaced by locomotives from other constituents of the LMS. On at least one occasion an ex-L & NWR 0-8-0 was employed, this being engine no. 9294 one day in 1926. Ex-L & NWR goods engines were rare along the line North of Marsh Lane

Junction, but in the inter-war years passenger engines from the L & NWR often hauled excursions to Southport. Finally, steam locomotives never seemed to be at home on this intensively-worked electric railway and were the subject of interest and comment on the part of passengers.

With the relentless passage of time, relics of Pre-Grouping days are very few along the Liverpool-Southport line nowadays. The old L & Y car bodies which were used for various purposes here and there have completely vanished. During 1942 an ex-L & NWR low-roof corridor coach (LMS No. 6052) stood in Crosby coal sidings for several months, and at the latter end of the year was hauled to Hall Road, taken off its bogies and installed at the rear of the car maintenance depot. It did not remain there long however, as it had gone by 1947. The body of a former Midland Railway goods van survived in Waterloo goods yard until the early 1960's, whilst similar demounted M.R. vans existed at Seaforth and Birkdale (there were two at the latter place). Notice plates headed LANCASHIRE & YORKSHIRE RAILWAY can still be found at some stations and level crossings, otherwise in most respects the Liverpool-Southport line is entirely modern.

Strangers at Southport, Chapel Street station on Saturday, 13th April, 1985. The last two Class 503 Wirral units on a farewell rail tour of the Merseyrail system, after which they were taken out of service. The tour was organised by the Railway Correspondence & Travel Society and the Locomotive Club of Great Britain. (Photo: S.G. Jones)

L&Y "Barton-Wright" 0-4-4 Tank engine as used on the Liverpool-Southport line until the introduction of the Aspinall 2-4-2 Tank engines with which they shared the work until the line was electrified. Engine No. 14 was built in 1886 and lasted until 1921, being the last one in ordinary service. Photographed at Liverpool Exchange station in 1902. (Photo: J.Ward collection)

Ex-L&Y Aspinall 2-4-2 Tank engine No. 50746 at Southport in its last days, being employed on station pilot duties. This type worked Southport line trains between 1889 and 1904. (Photo: J. Ward collection)

The Beeching Era and Afterwards

The descriptions of the electric lines earlier in this essay applied to the early 1960's, but since that time numerous and far reaching changes and developments have taken place. Closures of goods and coal yards have already been referred to, but much more has happened besides these melancholy events. New developments in the Marsh Lane area of Bootle caused the renaming of Marsh Lane & Strand Road station to that of Bootle New Strand in March, 1967, in order to identify it with the new shopping precinct that now covers acres of land formerly occupied by old narrow streets of terraced houses and small industrial buildings. At Liverpool Exchange station the separate ticket office for the electric lines was closed and tickets for all the station's train services issued from the remaining office, which formerly dealt with the main lines only.

In order to enable the closure of signal boxes during the night to be effected, it was decided that level crossing gates would be left open to the railway after 11.00 p.m. instead of the boxes being manned overnight as they used to be. Indeed, there was a move to abolish gates altogether at the crossings and replace them by automatic half-barriers. This was actually done at Crescent Road, Birkdale, in November, 1967, but opposition from people living elsewhere along the line caused postponement of the scheme for a few years. More recently barrier type crossings have been installed at Waterloo, Hall Road, Freshfield and Ainsdale, and the process is continuing.

A move that caused some dissatisfaction among the local populace was the closure, in March, 1967, of the level crossing at Hightown station and its replacement by a new road overbridge which involved a detour — no obstacle to motorists but a bind for pedestrians, who now had a lengthy walk to cross the railway. Car drivers were pleased of course, but people on foot were not kindly disposed towards the new arrangements. Protests were made, but to no avail and the level crossing remained closed and nobody allowed to cross the line there, even though the adjacent signal box remained open. The battle was eventually won by the residents however, as a footbridge was later provided.

The South Junction signal box at Southport was damaged by a gas explosion late in 1966, so the opportunity was taken to abolish it and close the South Easterly section of the triangle (the Southport Fork line). The track was removed after laying out of use for a time. Certain operations at Southport were somewhat hamstrung after closure of this useful line, as any train coming from the Liverpool direction destined for the Wigan line and vice-versa, had to run into Chapel Street station and reverse direction. Special trains only would be involved in this proceedure, of course. Even the coal yard shunting engine had to do this, but today there is no such working. The diesel train sets which replaced steam trains on the Southport-Wigan-Manchester service do not need to be turned on the triangle, as the driver simply changes ends as with electric trains.

A number of strange electric multiple-unit trains made their appearance in Southport during 1966, but they were not for passenger service. The trains concerned were original London-Watford line sets which had been for some years employed on the Lancaster-Morecambe line, and had become redundant through that line having been converted to diesel train operation. The displaced electric trains had pantographs for overhead wire current collection instead of third-rail shoes, so had to be hauled to Meols Cop works at which they were stored for some time, and then broken up.

From Sunday 18th June, 1968, all crossovers at Sandhills were rendered inoperative making the Southport and Ormskirk lines virtually two separate railways, connected only at Liverpool Exchange! A great onslaught was made also on the numerous auxilliary lines and sidings at Sandhills and Bank Hall, leaving an open, derelict desert where before, hundreds of goods and mineral wagons had been part of the daily scene. The extreme West pair of lines past Bank Hall station (not serving platforms) became sidings for a while but were subsequently removed, as also were the sidings on which electric trains were stabled. A long loop line between Bank Hall and Bootle, on the Down side, was also removed. At a later date the two West-side main lines serving the Down island platform were de-electrified and subsequently used only by the few goods trains serving what remains of the once vast group of sidings in the Sandhills area. Today only the Up side island platform remains in use at Bank Hall. The signal box here was demolished as part of these alterations, and colour-light signals had replaced semaphores along the whole section of railway between Liverpool Exchange and Bank Hall station by 1967. Signalling on the line between Liverpool and Bootle Junction, also Kirkdale has been operated from a new power installation at James Street station (ex-Mersey Railway) since the completion of the Link Line in May, 1977, of which more later.

The forgoing notes on economies make a sad tale, but what improvements have been carried out along the electric lines in recent times? In 1970 a programme of demolishing station buildings was commenced in the Liverpool area, mainly at the larger multi-tracked stations. The enormous mass of glass roofing and iron columns were removed from that most gloomy station of them all — Bank Hall, and a small modern-style shelter was built on the Up platform. The original waiting rooms were left intact on the Down platform, but this was subsequently put out of use. The removal of the roofing let in the sunshine and dispelled most of the gloom, and the station looks all the better for it. The brick booking office remains in use on the overbridge in Bank Hall Street however. The removal of roofing and column supports was also carried out at Bootle and Seaforth, though at Bootle some of the old buildings in L & Y yellow brickwork have been retained on the Up platform, a small new shelter having been built on the opposite platform. Seaforth actually lost most of its massive timber buildings at an earlier date — in 1963, but was later rebuilt and reduced to a single island platform with only a small bus-stop type shelter.

Surprisingly, Waterloo station retained its original platform buildings and awnings until late 1975, when they were replaced by a new and quite commodious waiting room, but the street level building on South Road bridge remained. Blundellsands & Crosby station lost all its original buildings but quite large new ones have been erected on each platform. Hall Road station retains its original buildings on the Up side, those on the Down side having been replaced by a small shelter. The same has happened at Hightown, but Formby, Freshfield, Ainsdale, Hillside and Birkdale remain unaltered. The complete metamorphosis at Southport Chapel Street has already been mentioned.

On the Ormskirk line, Kirkdale station, once sited amid busy rail traffic with running lines, loops, carriage and goods sidings etc., now stands in a partially derelict area with large tracts of empty land, but the recent building of the electric train depot has brought the West side of the line back to life. The steam locomotive depot has gone, as also have the two signal boxes, along with the once numerous semaphore signals. The station itself has been stripped of its awnings and the ancient brick waiting rooms partially modernised. Only one entrance remains, on the Down side on which a new concrete stairway has been built leading to the footbridge which has had its roofing removed and is now open to the elements.

Walton Junction, now renamed simply as Walton, and Orrell Park stations remain much as they were, and so also do Aintree, Old Roan, Maghull Town Green and Aughton Park. Electric trains are no longer stabled at Aintree, whilst very few freight trains are seen there nowadays. Like the Southport line, that to Ormskirk is mainly a passenger facility today, and there is little prospect of future development so far as goods traffic is concerned.

During the year 1972 vast works at Seaforth in connection with the new docks and container base completely altered the visual aspect of the district. A new motorway to serve the docks was projected Eastwards from the Mersey, and this intersected the Liverpool-Southport line immediately North of Seaforth & Litherland station. Consequently a long-span bridge had to be provided and this was constructed alongside the railway. It was rolled into position on Saturday night/Sunday morning on 25th/26th June, 1972. The existing plate-girder bridges over Seaforth Road were raised slightly as part of these works, and the old timber island platform, remnant of the once four-platformed passenger station, was replaced by a new one in concrete. An extension of the same motorway passes beneath the Ormskirk line North of old Roan, a lengthy new railway bridge being provided.

Withdrawal of the Liverpool-Aintree via Ford, and Crossens train services coupled with cuts on the remaining lines resulted in depletion of the rolling stock fleet. By 1967 seven of the 1939 type cars had been scrapped — some are believed to have been hauled all the way to Norwich, in Norfolk, to be broken up in company with many steam locomotives and other rolling stock. Further withdrawals took place later, and by 1977 the fleet consisted of 40 motor, 40 driving trailer and 36 trailer cars. When the Link line was built in later years, the rolling stock that was disposed of would have been very useful, as there was a perpetual shortage when that line came into operation, and resources were stretched to the limit.

In addition to the forgoing, Liverpool Exchange Junction signal box was closed and demolished in September, 1969, and crossover tracks disconnected, and it seemed like the end for the ancient viaduct of the original line to Great Howard Street used for goods only since the 1870's. but subsequent events changed the picture, of which more later.

After closure of the Southport-Preston line and the Crossens train service the direct curve between Hawkshead Street and Roe Lane Junctions was abolished, its track thereafter serving as sidings for the electric train workshops for a short while. Trains proceeding to the works ran to Meols Cop station at which they reversed and then travelled to Roe Lane, at which a further reversal enabled them to reach the works sidings. Eventual closure of these works has already been mentioned.

Now that the Liverpool-Southport and Ormskirk lines carry passenger traffic almost exclusively, they have become purely rapid transit facilities on a par with the London Transport system. Happily, the threats and black future that faced both lines in the 1960's did not become the reality that they nearly did, and the trains continued to run. Government grant aid for socially necessary train services largely saved the situation, and the formation of the Merseyside Passenger Transport Authority in 1969 saw the trend towards abandonment reversed. Once more rail advertising appeared in the Southport holiday brochures, cheaper off-peak facilities and unlimited travel tickets for specified periods were introduced. Bus and train interchange at various stations plus car parking facilities were made available, and a new group name for Merseyside local services was coined in order to build up a new image, thus the system is now known as MERSEYRAIL, of which the Southport and Ormskirk lines became the Northern Line of the group, which also has a City Line and Wirral Line.

Not only has a real attempt been made to infuse a new spirit into the local railways, but one or two schemes of ancient conception, periodically taken out of the files and put back again, came out again for action at last. The first of these, the Terminal Loop, a deviation from the original Mersey Railway in the form of a loop serving Exchange, Lime Street and Central stations has been constructed. The second one was the old proposal to join the Southport line to the Wirral lines so that trains could run through to the Cheshire side of the Mersey from North of the city, but this scheme was latterly modified in the light of studies concerning traffic trends, and the plan adopted instead has resulted in the Southport and Ormskirk lines being connected to the ex-Cheshire Lines tracks near Liverpool Central station, and the connection, in tunnels, is known as the Link Line. The CLC line has been electrified as far out as Hunts Cross, with an extension to Hough Green to follow. Interchange between the Link Line and Wirral line (the Loop Line) has been provided at the new Moorfields station which has replaced Liverpool Exchange.

The Parliamentary Act for the Link Line was granted on 27th July, 1971, and preliminary work put in hand during the following year. The Contractors for the scheme were C.V. Buchan & Company Limited. Main constructional work commenced in February, 1973 with the clearing of Great Howard Street goods yard, which had been used as a car and lorry park since 1964, and the moving-in of plant and stores. Soon the old yard lost all resemblance to its former appearance. The huge goods shed was not however, demolished until early in 1975.

Preliminary work at Exchange station had begun in November, 1972, with the extension of the engine lay-by siding on the East side, new track being laid on ground from which rails had been removed in 1965. This extension was required to partially compensate for the two Leeds Street sidings which were later obliterated in order to allow for the construction of a roadway to enable lorries, bulldozers and other vehicles to gain access to the work site. In addition, the non-electrified lines inside the station were equipped with third-rails to give more stabling accommodation for electric rolling stock, and later, for the arrival and departure of electric trains. Commencing on 5th May, 1973, platforms 8, 9 and 10 were taken out of use and the rails removed. From that date the Southport trains used platforms 6 and 7 and the Ormskirk trains, cut to two-car sets made up of a motor and a driving trailer, used platform 5, leaving the diesel trains on the Bolton service to platform 4. This arrangement involved inward and outward Southport line trains using a common stretch of single line for a few yards as a result of track removals, and there was some delay on the first day, but the new method of working soon became established and proved generally satisfactory. From 26th December, 1973 the double track out of Exchange on the West side of the viaduct formerly used by Southport trains, was taken out of use between

Exchange and Sandhills, and all the trains concentrated on the East side lines. For a short distance near Exchange the Down Southport line was used as a headshunt.

Track and signalling alterations and rebuilding of Sandhills station commenced on 17th December, 1973. In its new form Sandhills station has become an island platform only, with one track either side, the two outer platforms having been dispensed with. A new junction to the North of the station is the point of divergence of the Southport and Ormskirk lines. The rebuilt station was opened in September, 1974 and has been transformed from the most decrepit to the most modern intermediate station on the line.

The new Link Line takes the following course: From the site of the former Liverpool Exchange Junction at Clegg Street, it is laid on the original arched viaduct of 1846 which, after standing derelict for nearly a decade has been extensively overhauled and some lengths of crumbling parapet remade with concrete instead of bricks, a process which has spoiled the appearance of the structure considerably. At the site of the old wagon hoists in Great Howard Street goods yard, a ramp has been constructed, which leads directly into a cutting that has been excavated through the yard area, and takes the double track line to the tunnel portal below Leeds Street, nearby the enormous JM Centre building. The tunnel, which is actually twin bores side by side, runs through to Central station, the new section breaking into the original Mersey Railway tunnel beneath Paradise Street (the Mersey line has an entirely new tunnel, the Loop Line). Thus the Southport and Ormskirk trains terminate in the old Central Low Level platform formerly used by the Mersey line trains. Interestingly, the new line passes over the great arch of 1849 at Great Howard Street, the flooring of this structure having been strengthened with concrete for its new role — taking fast, frequent train services such as it had never known before in its 120 years plus existence!

The extensive works connected with the construction of the Link Line were largely completed during April, 1977, except for the installation of the main escalators at the new station in Moorfields. Final tasks involved with new signalling, and the linking up of new and existing lines, necessitated trains being terminated outside the city on the last couple of Saturdays and Sundays prior to the opening of the Link Line, bus connections being provided to and from Exchange station. A six-car electric train for test purposes and driver training was run through the Link Line tunnel during April, this train being on track that was as yet physically isolated from the main lines, and could be reached only via Birkenhead, by means of the main Mersey Railway tunnel and the connection between Loop and Link Lines beneath Lord Street.

The practice of running two-car trains on the Ormskirk line in the off-peak periods ceased early in 1977, and three-car sets were reintroduced, strengthened to six during the morning and evening rush hours. The electrification of the line between Walton Junction and Kirkby, opened concurrently with the Link Line, took the electric trains into new territory, the Liverpool-Bolton diesel trains which formerly covered that section of line being terminated at Kirkby, which became an interchange station, rebuilt and with the electrified line separated from the continuation to Wigan and Bolton by buffer stop-blocks as was done at Ormskirk. Through running (as at Ormskirk) is not possible here, as no loop is provided.

The derelict sites of the former Bank Hall locomotive sheds and the West side carriage sidings at Kirkdale took on a new lease of life due to the Link Line project, with the construction of an electric train stabling depot of quite large proportions, but this was not complete at the time the train services came into operation.

The great changeover took place on Monday 2nd May, 1977, when the first train to carry passengers over the new line left Liverpool Central station at 6.05 a.m. Many people left their beds early in order to be on this train, and each received a certificate from British Rail to celebrate and form a memorial to the event. Exchange station had been closed to rail traffic from the previous Friday evening, trains being terminated at outlying stations with bus links to and from the city so that engineering staff could carry out the task of connecting old and new lines at Liverpool Exchange Junction, or what had been its former site. It was a large and complicated task involving day and night work, and was completed on schedule.

The last electric train to depart from Liverpool Exchange station was the 11.05 p.m. to Ormskirk, the last arrival being a train from Southport due in at 11.38 p.m. The very last train of all was a diesel-locomotive hauled "special" for railway officials and interested members of the public, which was scheduled to depart at 11.32 p.m. and terminated at Lime Street. Thus one era ended and a new one began, the hurried tread of thousands of daily passengers, so characteristic of Exchange station for so many years, being replaced by silence and desertion.

New train schedules were introduced upon the opening of the Link Line. The weekday service to and from Southport was at 15-minute intervals throughout the day, augmented at peak hours, whilst the Saturday service was quite similar. The Sunday service (Summer) became basically every 15 minutes, with fewer trains in the early morning and late evening. The Winter service consisted of a train every 45 minutes or so. On the Ormskirk line the weekday service was at 20-minute intervals with extras at peak traffic times. The Summer Sunday service was a train every 30 minutes for most of the day, the Winter Sunday service being at intervals of 45 minutes. The new service to Kirkby provided a train every 20 minutes on weekdays, with peak-time extras, and a Summer Sunday service of a train every

30 minutes for most of the day. The Winter Sunday service is at 45-minute intervals. At first the Kirkby service was to and from Liverpool Central station, but was extended to Garston over former C.L.C. rails from 3rd January, 1978. Electrification onwards to Hunts Cross was completed in July, 1983.

The construction of the Link Line has ensured the survival and enhanced the usefulness of the Liverpool-Southport and Ormskirk lines, the former which came so near to complete closure during the "Beeching" era. Wiser counsels have since prevailed, and Liverpool, which had become an anti-rail city so far as local transport is concerned is once again in the forefront of progress! The steel wheel on the steel rail has moreover, at last been recognised as the ideal form of mass transportation. This is a source of considerable satisfaction on Merseyside, where the true railway age began, and is perhaps entering upon a second era. Far from dying and becoming nature trails and footpaths, the local railways will continue to play their part in the movement of Merseyside's legions of passengers, and it is likely that many years will pass before the rails begin to lose their silver shine, and the speedy, capacious trains replaced by another transport mode.

The only regular steam-hauled passenger trains to traverse the Southport line after it had been electrified were those between Southport and London (Euston) via Bootle Junction, Edge Hill and Liverpool (Lime Street), where the carriages were added to a Liverpool-London train, detached at Edge Hill on the Northbound journey. Here is one of the trains ready to leave Chapel Street station in August, 1932, hauled by ex-L&Y 4-4-0 locomotive No. 10110. (Photo: F. Dean)

Southport-London through-carriages hauled by 2-6-4 Tank engine No. 42233 on their way to Liverpool, where they will be attached to a train for London (Euston). March, 1966. Scene is near Hillside. (Photo: C. Whalley)

Northern Line extension to Hunts Cross. The official opening train arriving at Hunts Cross on 5th July, 1983. The train is a Class 507 unit.
(Photo: S.G. Jones)

Mileage Table — Passenger Stations

LIVERPOOL EXCHANGE-SOUTHPORT CHAPEL STREET

Liverpool Exchange	0	miles
Sandhills	1½	miles
Bank Hall	2	miles
Bootle, Oriel Road	2¾	miles
Marsh Lane & Strand Road (now Bootle New Strand)	3¼	miles
Seaforth & Litherland	4¼	miles
Waterloo	5¼	miles
Blundellsands & Crosby	6¼	miles
Hall Road	7¼	miles
Hightown	9	miles
Formby	11¼	miles
Freshfield	12	miles
Ainsdale	14¾	miles
Hillside	16¼	miles
Birkdale	17¼	miles
Southport	18½	miles

LIVERPOOL EXCHANGE-ORMSKIRK

Liverpool Exchange	0	miles
Sandhills	1½	miles
Kirkdale	2¼	miles
Walton Junction	3¾	miles
Orrell Park	4	miles
Aintree	5	miles
Old Roan	5¾	miles
Maghull	7½	miles
Town Green & Aughton	10¼	miles
Aughton Park	11	miles
Ormskirk	12¼	miles

LIVERPOOL EXCHANGE-AINTREE via MARSH LANE

Liverpool Exchange	0 miles
Sandhills	1½ miles
Bank Hall	2 miles
Bootle, Oriel Road	2¾ miles
Marsh Lane & Strand Road	3¼ miles
Linacre Road	4¼ miles
Ford	5¼ miles
Aintree	6¼ miles

SOUTHPORT CHAPEL STREET-CROSSENS. Direct Line.

Southport, Chapel Street	0 miles
St. Luke's	¾ miles
Hesketh Park	1¾ miles
Churchtown	2½ miles
Crossens	3 miles

Steamport Southport

Five minutes' walk from Chapel Street Station, Southport, brings you to the locomotive shed in Derby Road, since 1972 the home of Steamport Transport Museum. In this large late Victorian building there are several items from the local railway system. Cecil Raikes, the Mersey Railway steam tank engine, now almost a centenarian, awaits restoration. The signal cabin from Liverpool Riverside station, and a signal from Liverpool's dock area, are in full regular use, controlling the steam and diesel trains on their regular Summer Sunday and Bank Holiday runs along the Museum's own line.

The 1939 LMS electric coaches 28361 and 29896, in full running order, await repainting into LMS livery, hopefully in time for the 1986 celebrations. The Liverpool Overhead Railway trailer coach 7 contains some signalling equipment and other relics from that Railway.

Yorkshire-built diesel D2870, remarkably similar to British Railway's 02 class shunters at Bank Hall and Liverpool Docks, works regularly.

Liverpool's Baby Grand tramcar 245 is on display.

There is a wealth of photographic material on display, from the earliest LYR electric units and locomotives onward to recent times.

Steamport is open every weekend: it is also open on weekdays in July and August. Come and spend an hour or more reliving the scenes of the past; perhaps you will be inspired to join as a member, thus helping to keep the past alive — you will be very welcome.

Acknowledgements

This book has been written on the basis of my own experience, observation and note-taking of the lines concerned over many years, but for the historical background and technical details the publications listed herewith proved of great value.

Bradshaw's Railway timetables.
Electric Traction on Main-Line Railway *(Dick Kerr & Co. Ltd.).*
Herapath's Railway Journal.
Journal of the Stephenson Locomotive Society.
Lights Along The Line *(Henry Grazebrook).*
Liverpool Courier.
Liverpool Mercury.
Railway Magazine.
Railway Observer *(Railway Correspondence & Travel Society).*
Railways (later Railway world).
Recollections of a Busy Life *(Sir W.B. Forwood).*

For the long extinct and rare publications I am indebted to the Local History Department of the City libraries, Liverpool.

Illustrations

My grateful thanks to the following for their assistance in the supply of illustrations:

P. Bolger.
F. Dean.
Heyday Publishing Co.
S.G. Jones.
K. Longbottom.
J. Ryan.
G. Sarson.
R. Stephens.
C. Whalley.
J. Ward.